The
GURU'S SANDALS

Threshold of the Formless

The
GURU'S SANDALS

Threshold of the Formless

Swami Kripananda

A SIDDHA YOGA PUBLICATION
PUBLISHED BY SYDA FOUNDATION

Published by SYDA Foundation
371 Brickman Rd., P.O. Box 600, South Fallsburg, NY 12779, USA

Acknowledgments
I wish to express my gratitude to Ed Levy for his invaluable
help in editing the manuscript, to Marilyn Goldin for offering her
considerable talent to help in structuring and revising the text,
to Martin Epstein and Hans Tuerstig for checking the Sanskrit, to
Diane Fast for copyediting, to Cheryl Crawford for cover and text
design and typesetting, to Judy Heany for her contribution to
the cover illustration, to Angela Trinca for her painting of the
A-Ka-Tha triangle, to Leesa Stanion for compiling the index,
and to Sushila Traverse, Osnat Shurer, and Valerie Sensabaugh
for overseeing the production of this book.
— *Swami Kripananda*

Printed in the United States of America

02 01 00 99 98 97   5 4 3 2 1

Library of Congress Cataloging-in-Publication Data

Kripananda, Swami.
    The guru's sandals : threshold of the formless / by
Swami Kripananda
        p.   cm.
    Includes bibliographical references and index.
    ISBN 0-911307-54-0 (pbk. : alk. paper)
    1. Gurus. 2. Spiritual life--Hinduism. 3. Sandals. I. Title.
BL1241.48.K75   1997
294.5'61--dc21   97-26648
                                                        CIP

Permissions appear on page 90.

CONTENTS

DEDICATION

This book is dedicated to Swami Chidvilasananda,
at whose feet the wandering mind becomes still
and the heart finds its true home.

May I be worthy of the Guru's feet!
Through them I may attain all the goals of human life,
and through them I will gain that pure knowledge
that leads to rest in God.
— Jnaneshwar Maharaj

The Guru is Brahma.
The Guru is Vishnu.
The Guru is Lord Shiva.
The Guru is indeed Parabrahman.
Salutations to Shri Guru.

— Guru Gītā 32

FOREWORD

"Wherever my mind goes, may I see your beautiful form. Wherever I place my head, may I see your lotus feet." Ever since the Guru touched my life, I always remember this verse written by Saint Ramdas. Today, as I write the Foreword to *The Guru's Sandals*, I feel blissful. One should be addicted to studying the scriptures and savoring the sweetness of the Lord's feet. The book is divided into two parts, the first on the Guru and the second on the hidden meaning of the Guru's sandals. Both sections will be a great feast of knowledge for seekers.

The *sadguru* and the saints have only one purpose: to build an ideal character in all people. The Guru embodies generosity, auspiciousness, purity, greatness, contentment, compassion, and the longing for God. In the Guru there are no negative qualities such as hatred, jealousy, or greed. It is said that compassion and forgiveness are the servants of a saint. These great beings, who are without any selfish motive, are a source of inspiration for the whole world. Without the Guru, all knowledge and arts are not only incomplete but impossible.

This book begins with a discussion of the Guru

principle. In the *Mahānārāyana Upanishad*, it is said that all animate beings and inanimate objects are pervaded by the Consciousness of supreme Shiva. The Guru principle is the Consciousness of the primordial Guru, Lord Shankar, and that same Consciousness exists in each and every being. A being goes through many cycles of birth and death, experiencing both pleasant and unpleasant circumstances; then he finally attains a human body. In this birth as a human being, a person can be awakened to true knowledge and a longing for eternal bliss and contentment. Ultimately, one auspicious day, he meets the *sadguru*, or true Master. Once the Guru awakens divine knowledge in him, the seeker has different experiences of God's presence — in sounds, in visions, and even in his own friends. Because this Consciousness is universal and all-pervasive, one feels an attraction to places, to fire, forests, and stones.

The Guru is the cosmic power of grace-bestowal. There is a very beautiful analogy to shaktipat in the Upanishads. It is said that when dark clouds gather and lightning flashes, rain begins to shower on the earth. Those drops of rain nourish thirsty plants. The same thing happens when one receives shaktipat. Through shaktipat, a person who has grown tired of worldly experience and yearns for the experience of true bliss obtains showers of joy, and his ignorance is destroyed. Once a seeker receives shaktipat through the Guru's look, touch, thought, or mantra, his life is completely transformed. As a result of shaktipat, a person realizes his own true nature: he understands that he is a drop in the ocean of bliss. The Guru shows a seeker the way to merge with that ocean of bliss by constantly guiding him on the spiritual path. This book describes the work that the Guru's *shakti* carries out within the seeker's subtle body, removing its past impressions.

The subject of the Guru as the giver of knowledge is very beautiful. While studying the theme of devotion, one comes to know many remarkable things. The Creator of this universe contains within Himself the potential for infinite variety. He gives birth to millions of beings, but no one of them is exactly like any other. People have subtle differences in their voices, in their natures, in their handwriting, and so on. God has given valuable gifts to each human being. He has given one a great voice, another a sharp memory, and yet another inner inspiration. He has freely distributed thousands of arts, skills, and knowledge. But the amazing thing is that none of them are alike. There may be two singers who are equally famous, but they will each have different specialties in the music they sing. When the *sadguru* bestows his grace, divine knowledge arises within us and we come to know the unique nature of the energy we have been given. Once we find the key in the form of the Guru's *shakti*, we can experience constant bliss in our lives.

For many lifetimes we have nourished our desires, attachments, anger, hatred, jealousy, and lust. Our soul has become encased in different layers of impressions. The poet-saint Tukaram Maharaj says the physical body is the temple of God and the soul is God Himself who resides in this temple. In order to experience this, however, we have to get rid of the subtle impure impressions that have collected in the body and the mind. This means that the Guru's *shakti* must purify us, and this is yet another aspect of the Guru.

We can see the Guru interact with people in various ways: with children she becomes like a child, with adults she becomes an adult, and with the elderly she becomes an elder. But when we study the Guru principle thoroughly, we realize that the Guru is essentially all-pervasive light. Perhaps we may not understand this, at least in this one lifetime. However, the physical Guru is the embodiment of love and delight. Because of the Guru's nature, our process of purification is not difficult.

The theme of the Guru's *pādukās*, or sandals, is well worth contemplating. Even though Lord Panduranga used to talk with Saint Namdev and Namdev used to feed the Lord with his own hands, still one day in the company of saints, Namdev was declared an unbaked pot, unprepared for the path of knowledge because of his pride. Later the Lord commanded Namdev to find a Guru and take refuge at the Guru's feet. Only then was he able to fulfill his spiritual life and become a realized being.

Once you imbibe the knowledge of the Guru's sandals, humility comes to you on its own. All the saints have experienced that they attained everything without even asking, because within humility there are concealed so many treasures. This theme is very beautiful.

In order to understand the significance of the Guru's sandals, one must understand Shiva and Shakti. The Shiva principle is infinite and formless; it doesn't do anything. It is Shakti who creates all things and performs all activities. However, Shakti cannot do anything without Shiva. This universe becomes complete only when both Shiva and Shakti are present. From this point of view, the nature of the Guru's *pādukās* or sandals is very significant, for Shiva and Shakti reside in the *pādukās*.

While the person who is destined to become the Guru is still doing sadhana, he or she travels in the subtle body to all the different realms, such as the earth, the netherworlds, the heavenly region, and the plane of the ancestors. For this reason, the Guru has a store of merit in his feet or sandals. Moreover, the Guru has attained the power to destroy the fear of death and diseases of the mind and body. This same power also resides in the *pādukās*. For this reason, worshiping the Guru's sandals, we can easily attain all auspiciousness and blessings.

The entire science of mantra is based on *bījā* mantras, or seed letters.[1] In one place, the Vedas mention that throughout our physical body there is a very subtle arrangement that resembles a *vīṇā* or lute. Just as a lute has seven tones in seven specific locations, in the same way, our physical body contains all the *bījā* mantras in seven specific locations from the base of the spine to the crown of the head. When the repetition of the Guru's mantra makes the strings of the lute begin to resound, unknown inner melodies are awakened. The effect of this process is that one completely forgets one's hunger and thirst. Just as a gifted musician, through practice, gradually merges with the world of sound, in the same way, through the Guru's grace, a seeker's mind merges with the vibration of the mantra and the divine inner music, and becomes still in the Self.

While experiencing the primordial sound *So'ham* in meditation, a seeker can also experience the sound or vibration of the different seed letters and their surrounding mantras.[2] The sounds of these *bījā* mantras lead us to the *bindu*, or Blue Pearl, which is the ultimate goal. Sound is the path that takes us to the final destination. Just as a bee gathers honey from blossoming flowers, in the same way, the seeker savors the honey of the various lotuses, or chakras. Ultimately, the goal of everyone's sadhana is to attain liberation in the thousand-petaled lotus of the *sahasrāra* at the crown of the head.

This book also discusses the *a-ka-tha* triangle. It is said that *a* is the father of all letters. *Ka* is the seed of the *shakti* principle, which has the quality of a mother. *Tha* refers to the element of ether, which enables a seeker to soar like a bird in the inner space of Consciousness. A seeker attains this triangle of letters when he reaches the *sahasrāra*.

The ancient yogic scriptures also mention that within each human being there is a pot of divine nectar. When the seeker passes through all the different *bījā* mantras (the sounds of the lute) and rises from one chakra to another, after some time he reaches the lotus in the throat. At this point, the seeker experiences *khecharī mudrā*,[3] which clears the passage to the *sahasrāra*, and the divine inner nectar begins to flow. At this point, the Guru and the disciple merge into each other, without any separation between them. It is as though the company of the Guru rubs off on the disciple, and the disciple himself becomes the Guru. When the unstruck sound of *So'ham* completely ripens in a seeker, he realizes that everything except this sound is vain and empty.

Truly speaking, although this subject is very interesting and worth studying, still it is difficult. However, Swamiji, by the grace of her Guru, has explained it in a very simple way. It is a great honor for me to write the Foreword to this book. I thank you and wish you all auspiciousness. *Sadgurunāth mahārāj kī jay!*

Vivek Godbole
Gurudev Siddha Peeth
Ganeshpuri, India

Vedamurti Shri Vivek Godbole was born in Maharashtra, India, into a traditional brahmin family. In the age-old tradition of young brahmin priests, he began studying and memorizing the Vedas from a very early age, learning the sacred rituals prescribed in them. He performs Vedic ceremonies at Gurudev Siddha Peeth and Shree Muktananda Ashram, in the Catskill Mountains of New York State.

PREFACE

In 1972 I received shaktipat while attending a program
at one of Swami Muktananda's meditation centers in
northern California. During the course of the following year, I had so many powerful experiences during
meditation of Baba and of the awakened *kundalinī* that
I decided to travel to India to meet Baba in his physical form. When I arrived at Gurudev Siddha Peeth,
the mother ashram of Siddha Yoga meditation in rural
Maharashtra, I suddenly found myself immersed in a
spiritual tradition that seemed timeless, whose roots
seemed to extend so deep into the past that they
appeared to vanish into other world-ages and cycles
of time. It was a path with great heart, rich in meaning and depth of feeling. As a Westerner, however, I
found many aspects of it unfamiliar. One of the rid-
dles that most intrigued me during that first contact
with Siddha Yoga meditation was the image of the
Guru's *pādukās*, or sandals, and all the layers of meaning that seemed to be embedded in them.

A hymn is sung to the Guru's sandals every morning in Siddha Yoga meditation ashrams before the
recitation of the *Guru Gītā*, and the sandals are also
placed on altars and worshiped with great reverence

and devotion. They are so abundant with meaning that it takes years for it to reveal itself. As time has passed, more and more levels of significance have become clear to me.

Some things were evident from the beginning. Even if you don't understand what the sandals are, you may feel their power. The Guru's sandals are potent transmitters of *shakti*, divine energy, and of grace in whatever form it is needed. They have the capacity to unlock fresh streams of inspiration and remove obstacles of all kinds. In my case, even the most stubborn instances of writer's block, for example, or niggling anxiety about one thing or another yielded to the grace emanating from the Guru's sandals, which I visited every day in the Temple. However, the mystical significance of the sandals is so profound and subtle that it takes a considerable amount of time to absorb it.

Some twenty years after my initial contact with Siddha Yoga meditation, one morning I sank into a deep state of meditation while sitting in Gurumayi Chidvilasananda's presence, having her darshan. Within a shimmering curtain of blue light, three luminous Blue Pearls appeared and formed a triangle. The triangle began to expand, and in its center stood the Guru's sandals. As I came out of meditation, I was aware of a powerful throbbing at the crown of my head. I had had a glimpse of the inner sandals of the Guru in the *sahasrāra*, the highest spiritual center in the human being, located at the top of the head.

I have come to realize that the Guru's sandals and

also the Guru's feet — another potent symbol in yoga — address the basic mystery at the heart of the Guru, at the heart of sadhana, and at the heart of the Guru-disciple relationship, and in a way, the mystery that is the hardest to grapple with: that the Guru is both inside and outside. The Guru's feet are not merely a physical reality, not only a reality on the subtle plane as well, but also a symbol and key to the most exalted experiences of yoga and to sublime states of consciousness. Just as the Guru's feet and sandals can release the experience of the inner worlds and the Absolute, just as they are a guide to deciphering the mystery of our inner nature, of the divine Reality contained within us, in the same way they are vessels that hold the most potent concepts of yoga, from the most esoteric to the most concrete. By understanding the power and the themes held in the image of the Guru's sandals and the Guru's feet, we can come to comprehend the great forces at play in sadhana and on the spiritual path.

Now at the threshold of this book, we are invited to cross another threshold — to a realm beyond time and space, name and form — and to explore a mystery that is indeed hard for the mind to comprehend.

The book is divided into two parts. The first part takes up the subject of the Guru, according to the four main attributes or criteria of the Guru as explained in the sacred texts of India. Of course, here we are talking about a *sadguru*, or true Guru, who is a Siddha, a realized Master — not about lesser teachers. It is important to make this distinction, for in India the general term *guru* simply means a teacher; there are music gurus, dance gurus, and many other kinds of secular gurus. But that's not what we are referring to here. We are referring to a spiritual Master of the highest caliber and qualifications, that rarest of beings who is able not only to teach disciples the ultimate mystical truths about the world and the inner Self, but also to give the experiences of sadhana all the way to ultimate liberation. Part One deals with the Guru principle, the universal Consciousness that exists everywhere, at all times, and in all things. It discusses the Guru as the grace-bestowing power of the Supreme, the giver of shaktipat *dīkshā*, or initiation. It examines the Guru's role as the giver of knowledge and explores the function of the Guru as the purifier, the compelling force behind transformation.

The second part of the book probes into the deep system of meanings and powers that reside in the Guru's sandals: *Hamsa* or *So'ham*, Shiva and Shakti, *bindu* and *visarga*, the lotus and divine nectar. It also discusses the supreme *bindu*, or Blue Pearl, and the *a-ka-tha* triangle. The Guru's sandals are a symbol that embodies all these aspects of the Guru, but they are far more than a symbol only: the Guru's sandals have the power to release the Guru's *shakti* and grace.

May the great Gurus of the Siddha lineage grant us their blessings, may we behold their light in everything and everyone, may our minds take refuge at their feet, and may they abide forever in our hearts.

Swami Kripananda
Shree Muktananda Ashram
South Fallsburg, New York
December 5, 1996

The Guru has led me home on the path of yoga.
Because of him, the sun of knowledge has risen
And I have become the Absolute while still in this body.
Oh, how could I ever forget the Guru's sandals?

The Guru is eternal, all-pervasive;
I meet him everywhere, at all times.
We are united in the supreme state of consciousness.
Oh, how could I ever forget the Guru's sandals?

— Samartha Ramdas

PART ONE

The
GURU

CHAPTER 1

THE GURU PRINCIPLE

~

When you establish a relationship with the Guru, Swami Muktananda used to say, you are establishing a relationship with your own higher Self. You are relating to one who has become the embodiment of an eternal and imperishable Principle that transcends all limitations, including time, space, and death, and which is our true nature. This is one of the fundamental teachings of the ancient Indian tradition.

The *Guru Gītā* says: "I bow to the *sadguru*, who is the bliss of Brahman and the bestower of the highest joy. He is the Absolute.[1] He is knowledge personified. He is beyond duality, all-pervasive like the sky, and the object of the great Upanishadic statement 'Thou art That.' He is one. He is eternal. He is pure. He is steady. He is the witness of all thoughts. He is beyond all modifications of mind and body and free from the three qualities of nature."[2]

The sacred texts of the Indian tradition speak of the *guru tattva*, or the Guru principle, saying that God, the Guru, and the innermost Self of all beings are one and the same thing.[3] Hearing this for the first time, many people in the West are flabbergasted. It astounds us because of our conceptions about what God is, what the Guru is, and what we ourselves are. More than likely, we have been led to believe that God — if we even believe that there is such a being — is separate from us. To some the word *God* recalls artistic representations of an old man with a long white beard in a distant heaven, a stern and judgmental figure, someone to turn to when times get bad just in case He might be willing to help us out.

Even though we may not be quite sure who or what God is, we are sure of at least one thing: God is not us. We know what *we* are: we are only too painfully aware of all our shortcomings and weaknesses. How could somebody like us possibly be God? And the Guru, on the other hand, appears to be yet a third party, one who sits on the seat of a lineage. The Guru looks more or less like us. Consequently, we project all of our own limitations onto him and assume that the Guru is a person like us with all of our baggage of concepts, feelings, and perceptions. In this way we become hopelessly muddled, and when we hear the basic teaching of the *guru tattva*, or Principle, we simply don't know how to think about it at all.

The scriptures and the great beings gently but firmly insist that these notions about God, the Guru, and ourselves are not only incorrect, but they are also the fundamental cause of all our suffering and difficulties. The sacred texts of India state that God, the Absolute, is pure Consciousness.[4] The soul of each individual is made up of that same Consciousness. This is what is meant by Swami Muktananda's teaching "God dwells within you as you." An ordinary individual in his or her ignorance has forgotten the divine nature of his own conscious Self and identifies with his body, mind, and personality. He or she thinks, "I am a man. I am a woman. I am a lawyer, a teacher, a carpenter. I am tall or short, fat or thin, intelligent or dull, happy or depressed."

However, the Guru is a being who has exploded these limitations within himself and has merged his identity with the Consciousness at his core. In fact, one of the scriptural qualifications of a Guru is that he be *brahmanishtha*, literally, "standing in the Absolute."[5] The Guru is this divine Consciousness, and not just in one body, but in every body. Wherever Consciousness is, the Guru is: all-pervading, all-knowing, all-embracing.

Revealing this truth is the Guru's role. Another classical way of putting it is that the Guru's role is to remove the darkness of ignorance and lead the disciple to the light of knowledge. Knowledge of what? Of the disciple's own nature, of his own soul. All of this is a divine play, the play of Consciousness. On the stage of the world, God appears to forget His own supreme nature and looks for God, and it is God who ultimately finds God.

The great poet-saint Jnaneshwar Maharaj said:

> Finding no joy in solitude, pure Consciousness assumes the forms of both Guru and disciple.
> Although the Guru and the disciple appear to be two, it is the Guru alone who masquerades as both.
> When a person looks at his reflection in a mirror, he knows that he is seeing his own face.

> If the eye could behold itself without the aid of
> a mirror, I could describe this sport of the Guru.[6]

When I received shaktipat initiation from Swami Muktananda, a whole new realm opened up inside me. I became aware of a presence within me, which I knew *had* to be me — after all, it was inside me — but I also recognized it unmistakably as that being outside me whom I had come to know and love as "Baba." So Baba, for me, was never just a figure on the outside. He was equally present within me. I didn't understand how or why this could be so; I simply knew that it was true. Intuitively, I was able to grasp what the *Guru Gītā* meant when it said, "The Guru is not different from the conscious Self."[7] However, time and again, Baba furnished me with the experience of this understanding — that he was one with that presence inside me, that Self.

In Gurudev Siddha Peeth in those days, the early morning *Guru Gītā* recitation was often held in the semi-darkness, in the Guru Chowk courtyard under the spreading mango trees and in front of the small front porch of Baba's house. I remember one morning I was feeling drowsy and dozed off in the middle of the chant, a habit that Baba strictly disapproved of. All of a sudden, I clearly heard a voice inside me say, "Wake up!" I sat up with a start and instinctively turned to look at the Dhyan Mandir, the main meditation hall that is now Baba's Samadhi Shrine. There was Baba, looking out of the window at me and sternly, though silently, shaking his finger.

At that time, my favorite darshans of Baba occurred

at 3:00 A.M. every morning, when he would come out of his small front door, sit on his porch, and call his three little dogs, Kush, Bhutto, and Gopal. They would come running and Baba would feed them biscuits. Baba was incredibly tender at that hour. One morning I was very tired and overslept. I had a dream in which Baba came to me and asked, "Aren't you coming to see me this morning?" I woke up with a start and looked at my clock. It was 3:00! I threw on my clothes and raced down the stairs to Baba's porch. Just as I arrived, I heard the click of his latch and out he came. He looked at me, chuckled, and nodded his head.

Nothing impedes the Guru's consciousness — his oneness with all things is unbounded. It isn't just that he is close to one disciple, or two, or a hundred. He is the Self of all. A girl that I knew in California had an elderly grandfather whom she loved very much. He was a distinguished old man in his nineties and very conservative. His granddaughter had never told him that she had a Guru because she was afraid that it would upset him. Yet Baba was such an important part of her life that she wanted to be able to share that with him. Finally, she decided on a course of action: she bought a small color photograph of Baba and took it to the home for the elderly where her grandfather lived. She simply showed it to him without saying anything.

Her grandfather studied the photograph with an expression of growing amazement on his face. After a minute or two he said, "Why, this is me! Where did you get this photo? I've seen him four or five times in my life, but always inside of myself. This is the first time I've seen him on the outside. This is me! This is my Self!"

Needless to say, the girl was even more astonished than her grandfather. She told him that the photo was of Swami Muktananda, her Guru, and then told him all about Baba and Siddha Yoga meditation. The old man, wonderstruck, stared at the photo and asked his grand-daughter if he could keep it. She pinned the photo to the curtain by the side of his bed, and he spent the rest of his days gazing at it with deep contentment.

Stories like these are a great mystery and a constant source of wonder. In fact, people often asked Baba how such things were possible. On one occasion, someone asked, "Baba, are you everywhere at once?"

Baba replied, "Why not? How can the Self be in one place and not in some other place? The Self is present in every place, in all things, in every object, and at all times. The Self exists in everybody. . . . The Guru is nothing but the Consciousness pervading every sentient and insentient object. There is a triangle in the *sahasrāra* at the crown of the head. In the center of the triangle there are two feet, *ham* and *sa*, and these are the feet of the Guru. So the Guru exists everywhere and in everybody. There is no individual in whom the Guru does not exist. In the many He is the One, and in the One He is the many."[8]

At this point a person might wonder, "But he was human, wasn't he? How can anyone in a human body be all-pervasive?" The great Sufi poet and mystic Jalal al-Din Rumi once described it this way:

> I've heard it said, there's a window
> that opens from one mind to another.
> But if there's no wall, there's no need
> for fitting the window, or the latch. [9]

This is the indescribable state of a being whose individuality has merged with God once and for all, and who has attained cosmic awareness. When a river flows into the ocean and becomes one with the ocean, it loses its small identity as a river and takes on all the majesty and grandeur of the ocean. This is what is meant by perfect surrender: one gives up one's ego, the narrow sense of self, and becomes the ocean of Consciousness.

In Baba's words, "As you grow, your individual identity is dissolved, and it expands to embrace the entire cosmos. Either through meditation or knowledge, you cease to look upon yourself as a limited person and you expand into infinity. . . .

"When you attain the state of God, then you become aware of everything. . . . If I want to know what is happening in the universe, I can know. But why should I bother? The state of God is such that you are always aware that you are everything. The state of God does not want just to keep looking outside at mundane life; it transcends mundane life. . . . The state of God is completely beyond these things."[10]

Some years ago Gurumayi visited Houston, Texas, and gave a series of evening programs. A few months before her arrival, she established a Chanting Cave in the Houston Center, a room where a tape of the mantra *Om Namah Shivāya* was played twenty-four hours a day. People could stop in at any time and chant quietly or meditate for a while before returning to the demands of their busy lives.

Shortly before Gurumayi's arrival in Houston, the telephone at the meditation center rang in the middle of the night. After a while, the woman who was acting as manager answered it sleepily. On the other end of the line was Gurumayi, who asked, "Have you checked the mantra tape in the Chanting Cave?"

"Yes, Gurumayi," the manager said, "we were just in there earlier this evening, and everything was fine."

"Go check again," said Gurumayi. "The mantra has stopped. Be sure it keeps playing."

The manager went into the Chanting Cave and discovered that the tape recorder had malfunctioned. And Gurumayi, who was hundreds of miles away in Oakland, California, was somehow aware that the mantra had stopped playing in that room in Houston.

The Guru lives in a dimension beyond limitations. As Jnaneshwar Maharaj wrote in his *Amritānubhava*, "The ordinary sky is bounded by the horizon, but the Great Sky of the Guru is limitless."[11] It is the Guru's task to raise us to his own state, to dissolve the boundaries of concept and structure that hold us captive within the cramped confines of the ego.

When Gurumayi was in Heidelberg, Germany, one of the people who attended the retreat was a science teacher in his middle forties. He is a devotee who thinks of himself as a solid, practical-minded person. One afternoon, he was resting in his hotel. He heard the sound of bare feet entering his room and opened his eyes. Gurumayi was beside him. She gave him a long, very beautiful visit, answering questions that had been preying on his mind. Then she blew on the top of his head, and he fell into a deep, but very lucid, state of meditation. After what seemed to be a few minutes, he opened his eyes.

" Is everything better now?" Gurumayi asked him.

"Yes, Gurumayi," he answered.

With that, she left the room. A few hours later, he learned that during the time she had been talking to him, Gurumayi had been across town at the Stadthalle, meeting all the German people who had been doing seva. At first, the science teacher flatly refused to believe this. He had touched the Guru's arm; he could have sworn she was flesh and blood. He decided there was only one thing to do.

That night after the program, he again asked Gurumayi one of his questions.

"I already told you," she replied calmly, and repeated the answer she had given him that afternoon, word for word.

The Guru is the embodiment of pure Consciousness and can assume a form at any place and at any time. When we pray to the Guru, we are not praying to an individual; we are praying to universal Consciousness, the all-pervasive *shakti*. The Guru's form gives us a connection to that cosmic realm, in which all shapes and forms arise and subside.

Baba once said:

> The *shakti* pervades the entire world, from east to west, from north to south, above and below. It

hasn't spared anyone. Although a disciple may be far away from me, the *shakti* is the same there as well as here. I have to lose myself in the *shakti*; only then does the *shakti* work everywhere for everyone. It is all-pervasive, but I have the switch to turn it on. Even though light bulbs are everywhere, the switch is over there. . . .

When a being loses himself in the light, he becomes a perfect Guru. God is of the form of divine light. If I lose myself in that light, then I have perfection and complete Guruhood. When we worship a Guru, we don't worship his physical body. We worship him with the awareness that he is the supreme and all-pervasive light.[12]

CHAPTER 2

THE
GRACE-BESTOWING
POWER

According to Kashmir Shaivism, the supreme Reality, Shiva, performs five functions: emanation, preservation, reabsorption, concealment, and the bestowal of grace. Emanation refers to the creation of the universe, which emanates from the Supreme in varying degrees of density from the finest, subtlest levels down to the solidity of the material world. What has been created is preserved or maintained by that same divine Reality. Should something end — whether it is a word or an individual life — it is understood as being dissolved or reabsorbed back into the same supreme Reality from which it came. Concealment, the fourth function of the Divine, is the state in which Lord Shiva retains the creation within Himself in a potential or seed form before remembering it or creating it anew. It is also the action by which the supreme Reality hides Himself in the world behind the veil of illusion, or *māyā*. Through grace, the fifth function of the Divine, He reveals the Self everywhere even as the play continues on eternally.

The Guru is the instrument through which the

Supreme bestows grace. The *Shiva Sūtra Vimarshinī* states that the Guru is the grace-bestowing power of God. This cosmic power of grace-bestowal occurs by means of a process called shaktipat *dīkshā*, or initiation. *Dī* means "giving," and *kshā* means "destroying." What is destroyed is ignorance of one's true nature, and what is given is realization of the Truth. The word *guru* itself implies this same function. The syllable *gu* symbolizes darkness and the syllable *ru* symbolizes light, so the Guru is one who leads his disciples from the darkness of ignorance to the light of knowledge. The Sanskrit word *shaktipāta* literally means "the descent of *shakti*," or divine energy, from the Guru to the disciple.

In this way, the Guru fulfills a specific cosmic function. Not every realized being is also a Guru. Guruhood is passed from the Master to a specifically designated disciple in a lineage through which God's sacred power of grace is transmitted to humanity.

Baba Muktananda once said, "The Guru is not the body. The Guru is the energy that flows through the body, so the Guru and shaktipat are the same. The Guru is not an individual being; the Guru is the grace-bestowing power of the supreme Lord. . . .

"The Guru is not merely a symbol of the supreme Principle, but actually a storehouse of the supreme power. Only if the power is there can he be called a Guru. If that power is lacking, he cannot be called a Guru."[13]

In the yogic tradition, the power of God that flows through the Guru is called *shakti*. The sages of India worship *shakti* as the great Goddess, the Divine

Mother of the world. She is the great energy, inextricably connected to Shiva, which enables Him to carry out the five functions. Shiva and Shakti, God and His Power, are inseparable; you never find one without the other. In the various Indian religious traditions, sometimes one is worshiped, sometimes the other, sometimes both.

Shakti is both within and without. She is the cosmic energy that has created the entire universe. In fact, it is Shakti who has become everything, shimmering into all the countless shapes and forms that we see around us, even things we consider inert and lifeless, such as buildings and rocks. Shakti has become the sun and illumines the world. She has become the clouds and sends down rain. She has become the earth and molds Herself into mountains and valleys, plants and trees.

The Indian sages tell us that when She opens Her eyes, the universe comes into being, and when She closes them, the universe disappears. The ancient *Rig Veda* contains a magnificent hymn called the *Devī Sūkta*, the "Hymn of the Goddess," in which Shakti speaks of Her transcendent nature in the following way:

> I am the ruling Queen, amasser of treasures,
> full of wisdom, first of those worthy of worship.
> In various places, the divine powers have set me.
> I enter many homes and take numerous forms.
>
> The man who sees, who breathes, who hears
>   words spoken,
> obtains his nourishment through me alone.
> Not recognizing me, he yet dwells in me.

Listen, you who know! What I say is worthy of belief. . . .

I breathe out strongly like the wind while clasping
unto myself all worlds, all things that are.
I tower above the earth, above the heavens,
So vast am I in power and in splendor![14]

Inside us, this great Shakti is the energy that makes our hearts beat, our lips move, and our minds think. She is the force that enables us to perform all our activities. And yet, She also has another aspect that is secret and dormant. In this form She lies quiescent in the center of the body, at the base of the spinal column. In the human body, Shakti is known as Kundalini, the "coiled one," because She lies coiled like a sleeping serpent. It is the work of this hidden aspect of Shakti to carry out our spiritual evolution and bring us to the state of enlightenment.

It is a great paradox: the *kundalini* power sleeping within us holds the key to the secret of existence, and yet we spend lifetimes without even knowing that She is there. We can go all the way through our finest universities, graduate with honors, accumulate an impressive string of degrees, and never even hear of Her. When Kundalini is in Her dormant, potential state, it seems as though we are bound and limited. We are frustrated and sometimes plagued by insecurity. Love eludes us. We vaguely suspect that there is this vast thing inside us, untapped, that we have no access to, and that until we unravel the mystery we will only be living half a life. We feel as though we are living on the surface of our being.

When I was in graduate school, almost every morning around four o'clock I would have the same dream: I was perched precariously on the rim of a giant wheel that was revolving in space, and I knew that I could fly off into infinity at any moment. What was it all about? It was many years before I encountered the Guru and the ancient wisdom of Kundalini, which taught me to slip down one of the spokes and take refuge at the hub of the wheel of life, at the core of my being.

When Kundalini Shakti is awakened, She begins to dissolve our limitations and brings meaning to life. She reveals the realms that exist within us, waiting to be discovered, and we come to understand our true greatness. She is the force that kindles spiritual understanding, the perfect energy of grace that brings us to liberation.

Gurumayi once said, "You can always tell the difference between a person who is initiated and one who is not. In a person who is initiated, the light is awakened, and a splendor shines throughout the body, the mind, and the intellect."[15]

It is a tremendous thing to give shaktipat and awaken Kundalini, and this is the task of the Guru. The Guru is not just a teacher who makes us learn a few facts; the Guru is not just someone who instructs us in a few hatha yoga *āsanas*. The Guru is one who can transmit God's power of grace and kindle the flame of Kundalini with the fire of his or her own blazing *shakti*. Few are they who have become so perfect and so pure that the undiluted power of God can run through them unimpeded.

Historically, the gift of shaktipat is extremely rare, and even a lifetime of spiritual practice does not guarantee this awakening. A very moving incident took place some years ago in Gurudev Siddha Peeth. A yogi came to meet Baba and to have his darshan. He was a distinguished older man with a kind face and gentle manner. He told Baba why he had come: for twenty years he had been practicing *ashtānga yoga*, the classical eight-limbed yoga set down by the sage Patanjali, but he had never had an experience of the inner Self. "I just can't quiet my mind," he told Baba. "Can you help me?"

With great understanding and compassion, Baba took him to the small interior room within the Dhyan Mandir where Baba had practiced intense mantra repetition for many years. Baba put him inside, gave him some instructions, and closed the door. Several hours later, the man emerged; his face was transformed and there was light in his eyes. He went to Baba, bowed, and with tears in his eyes said, "Oh, Baba, if only I had met you twenty years ago! What wouldn't I have attained by now?"

It is only through grace that we can enter the spiritual path and attain divine knowledge. Seekers from all traditions and in all times have discovered this fact. Their stories, though different in terms of detail, all share a certain similarity: an ordinary person meets the Master and is overwhelmed by grace. His awareness changes and his life is transformed, sometimes subtly and sometimes dramatically.

When Gurumayi was in Phoenix, Arizona, a lovely

Roman Catholic nun came to meet her. As a young girl, this nun had so much love for Jesus that at the age of thirteen she boarded a train and went to a convent in Arizona to give her life in service. But with the passing of the years, her heart began to dry out. When she met Gurumayi, she was thirty-seven years old, and she was seriously questioning whether or not she should leave the convent. She took an Intensive, the principal program of Siddha Yoga meditation during which Gurumayi gives shaktipat, and she had the most profound experience of Jesus that she had ever had. It completely reconnected her to her own tradition. With great joy, she resumed her teaching duties at the convent, and whenever she had some vacation time, she would spend it with Gurumayi.

Baba strongly emphasized the necessity of awakening Kundalini. On one occasion he said, "The scriptures say that as long as the inner *kundalini* is sleeping, it doesn't matter how many austerities we follow, how much yoga we practice, or how many mantras we repeat, we will never realize our identity with our inner Self. We will never know our own divinity, or understand God, or experience the all-pervasiveness of Consciousness. In our present state, we identify ourselves with this body which has a certain size and shape. We are not aware that we are all-pervasive. It is only when Kundalini is awakened that we become aware of our true nature, of our greatness, of the fact that not only do we belong to God but we *are* God."[16]

In whatever form it may occur, shaktipat involves

a transmission of energy from the Guru to the disciple, and this awakens the seeker's own dormant *kundalinī* energy. Traditionally, the Guru may do this in four different ways: by a look, a word (classically, the mantra of the lineage), a touch, or by his thought or will.[17] Sometimes shaktipat may take place before a seeker knows anything about it or understands what it is.

Who knows what yearning or what destiny draws the grace-bestowing power to a seeker? Over the years, many devotees have shared with me how they came to the path of Siddha Yoga meditation and what led to their receiving shaktipat. And each story is astonishing; each seems to have the thread of a miracle in it. Sometimes people search for years before they find the Guru; at other times, without being aware of seeking, they seem to collide with this divine force, and it changes their lives.

How is it that the Guru is human and more than human? How has he erased his own limited individuality so there is this empty space through which God flows? Such a being has usually spent many years as a disciple of his own Guru. He has gone through a gradual and lengthy process of surrender and expanding consciousness that continues over the years as the narrow ego is worn down, slowly but surely, through intense spiritual practice and selfless service to his Master. His own individual will is gradually brought into alignment with the divine will as he opens more and more to the vast Consciousness that is the Guru. If a seed does not surrender to the earth on which it falls, it withers and dies. But if the seed surrenders to the moisture and the soil and opens itself to a greater force, then it grows into a tree.

The Guru's all-encompassing state is the culmination of the process of spiritual unfoldment that is initiated with the awakening of *kundalinī*. The Guru must have attained the state of union with the omnipresent *shakti*, for in addition to bestowing grace and awakening the divine energy, the Guru must be able to direct the intensity of its functioning in the disciple throughout the seeker's sadhana. This capacity is of the utmost importance and is a criterion that the disciple must not overlook when seeking a Guru.

Once a woman began to feel pain in the area of her solar plexus. She had been experiencing a lot of fear and thought that the pain was associated with anxiety. Usually it came and went, but one evening the pain intensified and a knot formed in that area. She went to bed scared, not knowing what to do. She prayed to God for help and surrendered to the possibility that she might have to go to the hospital. The thought frightened her, and she felt very alone. Eventually she fell asleep and had a dream.

In the dream, she was standing behind a woman who was having Gurumayi's darshan. She noticed that Gurumayi was sitting with her arms folded over her abdomen. The next thing she noticed was Gurumayi's feet. She had never understood anything about the Guru's feet and had wondered, in India, at the great reverence shown the feet of the Guru. But in this dream she knew that, if she wanted to, she could touch the Guru's feet. When it was her turn to *pranām*, she placed her head on the big toe of Gurumayi's right foot. She felt a great deal of heat going into her head from Gurumayi's toe. When she got up, Gurumayi smiled gently at her and looked away. She was still holding her arms over her abdomen.

The next morning when the woman woke up, the pain and the knot in her solar plexus were gone. She realized that the Guru had taken them away. She understood that the pain and the knot were actually fears that had accumulated over many years. They were fears that she could not process consciously and could not name, but she knew she needed to be free of them. To this day, she says, the pain has not re-turned, and she is less fearful than in the past.

Shaktipat gives us a permanent connection with divine grace, which is always with us during difficult times and which often takes the form of consolation. It protects us from fear and from harm. The Guru is the one great energy that flows through everyone and everything. It is indivisible and does not lose its unity by becoming the universe. This is why it often seems as though the whole universe conspires to come to the aid of those seekers who have received the Guru's grace.

Seemingly magical events happen around the Guru quite frequently. As Baba used to say, divine powers come unbidden and dance in attendance on such a being; they are constantly engaged in serving him and stand before him with folded hands. For this reason, many people come to the Guru for grace and blessings — blessings to find a husband or wife, to have a child, to win a court case, to find a better job, to pass a difficult exam, or to recover from an illness. There is nothing wrong with this, really. The Guru sometimes grants us our desires so that we will come to desire the highest for ourselves. As the great saint Sai Baba of Shirdi said, "I give people what they want, in the hope that one day they will want what I have to give."

Yet the true wealth of the Guru's grace is the knowledge of our own divinity. Baba said, "The Guru's grace is the inner awakening. It is called Guru's grace when you attain the love of God. As man continuously revels in the external world, his inner path is blocked. . . . He can neither understand himself nor others, nor can he experience any peace. Through the Guru's grace, the inner path is opened. Then man enters within and finds the abode of peace. When this happens, he understands himself and others, and his life is filled with bliss."[18]

Shaktipat transcends all religions; it is not the monopoly of the Indian tradition. It has been known throughout history to the esoteric branches of all the world's great religions and to the poet-saints and mystics the world over. Once we receive shaktipat, we are given the key to understanding the world's great mystical literature. It is as though we inherit the grace of all the saints in all places and at all times.

When I received shaktipat from Baba, waves of divine love began to surge through me with tremendous intensity. Immediately, I remembered the Spanish mystics whose works I had read in graduate school —

Saint John of the Cross, Saint Teresa of Avila, Fray Luis of Leon. At the time, I had been unable to relate to them at all and found them tedious, a bit dusty, and out of reach. But now, suddenly, I understood with great clarity what they had been talking about. Divine love was an immense and astonishing reality. I devoured stories of the Ba'al Shem Tov and the Sufi Masters, as well as the great beings and *avadhūtas* of India.

A woman I know, a well-known Mexican poet, said that after she received shaktipat she developed a newfound interest in the pre-Hispanic cultures of her homeland; for the first time she could feel the spiritual power in their sacred places.

Grace creates a revolution within us. As our inner path to the Self begins to be cleared, our way of seeing things changes. We feel at one with nature and sense our kinship with all people. We become aware of the holiness of life. Shaktipat is a gift beyond compare, the gift of divine grace bestowed by the Guru.

The *Kulārnava Tantra* says:

> Shiva is all-pervasive, subtle, beyond the mind, without attributes, imperishable, eternal, and infinite. How can such a one be worshiped? That is why, out of compassion for His creatures, He takes the form of the Guru and, when worshiped with devotion, grants liberation and fulfillment. . . . The Guru is supreme Shiva clothed in flesh, who walks the earth, concealed, bestowing grace.[19]

CHAPTER 3

THE GIVER
of KNOWLEDGE

The sacred texts say that a Guru must be *shrotriya*, learned in the scriptures. This is a qualification that enables him to teach disciples. The word *guru* implies a teaching function: a Guru will always have disciples, to whom he imparts divine knowledge. Scriptural knowledge gives one a standard by which to measure one's spiritual experiences; to be legitimate, they must accord with the Truth as revealed in the holy writings.

As Gurumayi once said, "When you are seeking the Truth, you have to know what the Truth is; you cannot be hazy about it, you cannot be unclear about it. You have to know. You have to know it either from the wisdom of the scriptures or from the wisdom of the great Masters — the wisdom of those people who have attained the Truth. Believe in their experience, in what they have attained, so you have that clear picture of the Truth. And then, with that as your goal, you proceed on the path." [20]

For this reason, Gurumayi lectures tirelessly wherever she goes, as did Baba before her, basing her teachings on her own direct experience of the Truth, which makes her able to understand and interpret the scriptures in the way that few can. One of the *Shiva Sūtras* says, "The constant dissemination of divine wisdom is his charitable gift to humanity."[21] The Guru frequently communicates this highest form of knowledge in a traditional way through oral and written teachings.

Since the most remote times, in the *gurukulas*, or schools of wisdom of the Indian sages, disciples have received the Guru's sacred knowledge according to a threefold process: *shravana*, hearing the Guru's words, learning and memorizing the teachings; *manana*, contemplating what has been heard, asking questions, relating the teachings to one's own experience; and *nididhyāsana*, meditating on the teachings and imbibing their inner meaning.[22]

The *Taittirīya Upanishad* says: "The teacher is the first element, the pupil the second, and knowledge is their union."[23]

As we have seen, a Siddha Guru, or perfected Master, is *brahmanishtha*, "standing in the Absolute." Therefore, his thoughts, words, and actions flow directly from the highest state of Consciousness. As a scholar of Shaivism has said, "The Siddha . . . functions as a lively intermediary, a living spring through which the primordial and unspoken perception that the ultimate consciousness has of itself is able to emerge into language."[24]

This means that every word uttered by the Siddha Guru is empowered by the all-knowing awareness of pure Consciousness. It comes to us with the force of mantra, divine syllables that are the sound body of God. His every thought and word is a manifestation of the sacred. Moreover, because the Siddha Guru exists simultaneously in all places and has access to the hearts of all, in this way too he vastly transcends the scope and capacity of an ordinary teacher. His instruction is not confined to a classroom situation where he lectures and the students take notes. His methods and opportunities for teaching are unbounded.

During the early part of his Third World Tour, Baba visited Hawaii and stayed in a small house on Kahala Beach in Honolulu. In the evenings, he would give programs in a nearby school. One evening during his talk, Baba spoke about one of his favorite themes — that the Supreme has become everything and that all the different forms we see around us are actually composed of pure Consciousness. After the program, some of us returned to Baba's house and sat with him quietly in the living room. At one point, Baba gave me a long and penetrating look that set something spinning above the crown of my head. The sensation was that of a helicopter blade whirring, and it lasted all night long. I remember waking up occasionally during the night and finding the whirring sensation still there.

Early the next morning at 4:00, I got up as usual and walked along the beach from the house where I was staying to Baba's house. With Baba's permission, every morning I would slip in the back door, wait for him and Gurumayi to go on their morning *japa* walk to Diamond Head, and then sit for meditation in the small alcove behind Baba's chair in the living room.

That particular morning, as I repeated the mantra in preparation for meditation, the whirring intensified. Suddenly the wall in front of me, which separated Baba's living room from his kitchen, dissolved into sparkling blue energy and I could see right through it. I saw his two cooks in the kitchen making Baba's breakfast. They would take the juice and the bread out of the refrigerator and put the bread in the toaster. I saw that all those seemingly substantial objects — the juice, the bread, the refrigerator, and the toaster, as well as the cooks themselves — were simply clusters of shimmering blue light. I recalled Baba's talk from the previous night and realized that I was having a direct experience of the teaching that everything is composed of Consciousness.

In Baba's words, "Every day we see That, but still we don't have knowledge. Every day we hear about That, but still we don't understand. We are surrounded by that divine pure knowledge; we are wandering in the midst of it, but still we are not aware. We are like a boat in the middle of an ocean. Inside us and outside us, above and below us, behind us and in front of us, that Consciousness is all-pervasive. Consciousness is just like the ocean, and we are all the waves and ripples of that ocean. . . .

"You don't have to search for that Truth anywhere else. But through the grace of the Guru, through the love of the Guru, your real eye should open."[25]

There is a distinction between mystical wisdom and the kind of intellectual knowledge that we can acquire from books. Mystical knowledge is infinitely subtle, and there is nothing more profound. We are incapable of truly understanding the ultimate Reality as described in the scriptures until our experience has deepened to the point where we ourselves can see through the eyes of the sages.

It is for this reason that the scriptures and the religions of the East speak of opening the "eye of wisdom," the *ājñā chakra* at the space between the eyebrows. This is the *divya chakshu*, the divine eye, which we need in order to see into the terrain of sacred knowledge. Even before we become pure enough to sustain this subtle vision, the Guru gives us glimpses of it that uphold us and keep us going in our sadhana. That day in Honolulu, Baba gave me a direct experience of the Truth; he initiated it and guided it. The Guru teaches on all levels — from the most concrete, by delivering the teachings in a verbal form, to the subtlest, by giving us direct perception.

No matter how many books we study or how many lectures we hear, our knowledge remains at the intellectual level until we receive the grace of the Guru. Grace alone allows us to pierce through the veil of appearances and see the Reality that lies behind it.

The *Shiva Samhitā* says: "Only the knowledge which issues from the lips of the Guru is alive. Other forms of knowledge are barren, ineffectual, and the cause of suffering."[26]

In the physical presence of the Guru, knowledge is often imparted in subtle ways. Such a being is like a tuning fork: in the Guru's presence, we begin to vibrate with the same frequency. Baba used to explain that true darshan is to see the Guru and become absorbed in his state for a while. Then everything becomes crystal clear. A most powerful illustration of this is Baba's description in *Play of Consciousness* of his own darshans with Bhagawan Nityananda. He writes in great detail of how he would sit in his Guru's presence, meditate on him, and attain a state of oneness with him.

The knowledge that we gain from the Guru shines in the mind and the intellect, dispersing the shadows of misunderstanding and ignorance. Unlike the facts and information we receive from an ordinary teacher, the words of the Guru take root inside us and operate like light, enlivening and giving power to the teachings of the scriptures. The Guru's knowledge changes us: it changes our notions of who we are, what we want, and how we wish to live. It doesn't limit our choices in life; it gives us our freedom so that whatever we do, we seek to bring this knowledge into the center of it.

The Guru's teachings are often very down-to-earth and practical. One Sunday, a Texas lawyer went with a group of friends to a restaurant featuring southwestern-style barbecued ribs, a great favorite of his. He had one helping, then another. At this point his friends began to incite him saying, "I bet you can't eat any more!" He rose to the challenge and gobbled down thirty ribs. He went home after the party and was sick all night long. The next morning he was at his office, miserable, his head on his desk, when the telephone rang. It was Gurumayi, who was in South Fallsburg at the time. Though no one had told Gurumayi what had happened, she started the conversation by saying, "You shouldn't eat so much pork." The lawyer was amazed. As well as a lesson on his diet, he had received certain knowledge of the Guru's omniscience.

The scriptures may emphasize a life of discipline, but because they are inanimate, a seeker does not really have to surrender to them and observe what they say; he can interpret them in any way he finds convenient. But a seeker cannot interpret the living Master. As Baba expressed it, "You may change the scriptures, but the Guru will certainly change you."[27]

The Guru speaks outside us, and the Guru speaks inside us as well. Inwardly, the Guru's teaching may take the form of inspiration and spontaneous insight. Ultimately, the knowledge that we receive from the Guru is the understanding of the nature of Truth; it is recognizing the one great light that exists in everyone and everything. Gradually, in the course of our sadhana, we learn to perceive its radiance everywhere in the world. We nurture and protect this knowledge by doing the spiritual practices that the Guru gives us: meditation, chanting the divine Name, repetition of the mantra, contemplation, and selfless service. These practices help us to imbibe the Guru's teachings. If we become slack or negligent in our practices, our state suffers accordingly.

That happened a few years ago to someone I know. The man who was then the manager of the Honolulu Ashram let his spiritual practices slide and began to feel disconnected from Gurumayi, who at that time was on tour in Los Angeles. At one point,

Gurumayi began to call the Honolulu Ashram and ask to talk to everyone except him, and he became painfully aware of how bad his inner state had become. After this had continued for some time, one day, in anguish, he fell to his knees in front of his *pūjā* and said, "Gurumayi, help me. I need to be with you." The next day Gurumayi called and asked to talk to him. "Come to Los Angeles right away on the next plane," she said.

Some of the lessons that the Guru gives us are almost invisible at first. Occasionally, we think how easy it would be if the Guru would just come right out and say, "At this stage of your sadhana you have to do such-and-such a thing," or "I want you to understand this or that about your character." But would we really get it at a deep level? Would we take it to heart? Many times the most effective way the Guru imparts knowledge is by making us find our own way through a situation. Once we truly learn the lesson and imbibe it, the Guru immediately responds — not necessarily on the outer level. Most often the response comes from deep within.

Don't we often wish we could speed up the learning process? We become impatient and want instantaneous realization. We wonder why we aren't moving faster and become overly hard on ourselves. What we must remember is that spiritual unfolding, like many other things in life, is a process of ripening and maturation. If we want to eat an apple, it won't do us any good to snatch a blossom prematurely from the tree; we have to wait patiently for the fruit to form and become ripe. There are seasons to sadhana. The Guru is not only the master of the knowledge we seek, but also of the various phases of our growth. So before he can grant us supreme knowledge, the Guru must often show us our own ignorance.

What is crucial is to imbibe the Guru's teachings and make them come alive in our lives. Gurumayi once said, "To be a disciple doesn't mean you have to be very close to the Guru physically. You come very close to the Guru when you follow the teachings, when you take the words of the Guru to heart."[28] Therefore, we can give ourselves to the practices that the Guru gives us and let them ripen us — not just occasionally, but every single day, with dedication and commitment. Meditation gives us access to the state in which these teachings are revealed. The practices are the medium through which the Guru's knowledge and energy can unfold within us. The practices give us a connection to the teachings. They are the course of study of the Self.

In fact, the practices *are* the Guru. The Guru is the *shakti*, the power of the Self that infuses and enlivens the mantra. When we repeat that mantra, it permeates every one of our cells with its radiance and energy of enlightenment. The Guru is the power beyond the mind that cuts through the mind and plunges us into a state of deep meditation. When we give ourselves to the practices, the Guru becomes an ever-present reality inside and outside, which is a constant source of teaching and inspiration. The Guru may also appear to us in the form of an inner or outer vision to encourage us or give us a teaching. We don't have to be with the Guru's physical form all the time in order to receive the Guru's knowledge.

A woman I have known for many years is an artist, a housewife, and the mother of four beautiful children who are now grown and have families of their own. She met Baba in the mid-seventies and longed to be with him, but her family responsibilities made it almost impossible. In fact, Baba himself told her — as he did most parents — that her duty was to take care of her family with great love. So this woman devised a schedule that worked for her. She would get up early in the morning while her family was still asleep, and she would meditate and chant the *Guru Gītā* in a special area of her workroom that she had set aside for her spiritual practices. When her family woke up, she would fix their breakfast and get them off to work or school. She stuck to this schedule for many, many years with occasional, rare visits to take an Intensive with Baba and, later, with Gurumayi.

Several years ago she wrote me a letter saying, "You know, as I'm writing to you I'm looking out of my kitchen window, and I can clearly see Gurumayi sitting in my backyard. Whenever I drive to the supermarket or run some other errand, I see her walking ahead of me by the side of the road. And whenever I have a question, I sit down quietly and tell Gurumayi that there is something I need to ask her. Then she always appears in front of me, slightly to the left, in peach-colored robes. She leans forward slightly as she listens intently to my question, and then the answer always comes up inside of me — not in the form of a voice, but in the form of inspiration. It never fails."

I recently spoke with this woman on the phone, and she told me that Gurumayi continues to appear to her, but now on the inside instead of outside. What rich fruit her sadhana has borne! Her devotion to the Guru and dedication to her practices over the years have brought her great inner wealth.

CHAPTER 4

THE PURIFIER —
THE FORCE *of*
TRANSFORMATION

Another principal function that the Guru fulfills is purification. Both in his subtle form as the *shakti* and in his outer form as the Master, the Guru purifies the disciple in order to bring about a profound change in the disciple's inner state. As Baba once said, "The word *Guru* is of great significance; just on hearing the word the disciple should start feeling the transformation within. If there is no change in the disciple after meeting the Guru, if he remains the same as before, it would have been better if he had stayed at home."[29]

While some people experience radical transformation even at a first encounter, many others experience growth in a less dramatic or obvious way over a period of time. As we begin to apply the Guru's teachings, we notice a change taking place in our life. Baba continues, "One must become a new being. It is not a bond of friendship that you establish with the Guru, and therefore you do not choose him as you choose your friends. The Guru must awaken you to the Self in you. He must destroy the undesirable aspects within you."[30]

What aspects are undesirable? In terms of the

spiritual path, anything that keeps us from the experience of our divine Self must be purified. This can be compared to the process of distilling water or the operation of ridding gold of its dross. It is the process of transformation that begins within a seeker at the moment of shaktipat and the awakening of *kundalinī*. It is both natural and inevitable.

It is the understanding of yoga and the sacred texts of India that everything we have thought, said, and done has lodged within the *sushumnā nādī*, the central channel of the subtle body, through which the awakened *kundalinī* rises. These old past impressions are called *samskāras*, and we carry them around with us, being both burdened and influenced for good and for ill by this living past. These memories and impressions often spring into action like automatic reflexes. They are like tapes that play, causing us to act and react in certain set patterns. This explains why change so often escapes us, however much we may desire it.

When the Guru awakens *kundalinī* within us, the divine energy begins to expel these *samskāras* from our system. This is what Gurumayi means when she says, "The awakened fire within disturbs the burden of your destiny, and it slowly releases you from being trapped by the fruits of both your good and bad actions."[31] It is important to understand that this is the linchpin of the yogic notion of freedom: we no longer have to lug our past around with us. The *shakti* streams through all the *nādīs*, which run through our subtle system like veins, cleansing them and removing toxins and blocks. When this happens, some people experience *kriyās*, movements of the physical body inspired by the awakened energy. Though we experience them in our own individual way, they are classic signs of an awakened *kundalinī*, and down through the ages, Masters of the esoteric tradition of *kundalinī yoga* have described and categorized them: a person's body may sway, his head may shake, or he may spontaneously perform hatha yoga postures; the breath may be retained or brought in and out like a bellows. These *kriyās* occur only if one's body needs them, and their function is to remove obstructions and impurities in the system. Once the blockage is removed, there is no further need for that particular *kriyā*.

Other purifying manifestations of *kundalinī* are of a vocal nature. People may find themselves uttering mantras or words in Sanskrit or other languages that they have never consciously heard before. At other times they may make animal-like sounds. The yogic texts have classified the various manifestations of awakened *kundalinī* within four major categories: *kriyāvatī*, movements of the physical body; *varnamayī*, vocal manifestations; *kalāvatī*, purification of the gross and subtle elements of the body and the psyche; and *vedhamayī*, piercing of the chakras, centers of spiritual energy within the subtle body.[32]

There is also an emotional component to the purification governed by *kundalinī*. One may experience a sudden upsurge of negative feelings such as anger, lust, jealousy, hatred, and so on, as old patterns, images, and emotional triggers are churned up and released. At such times, it is important to remember that this process is a beneficial one, if not always pleasant. Old, deep-seated material emerges into our awareness on its way out of our system — unless, of course, we choose to cling to it and nurture the dark qualities instead. It cannot be stated too often that in the matter of transformation we are not passive bystanders. We either cooperate with this process, or we try to stifle it or slow it down.

As the negative qualities are gradually eliminated, our state becomes lighter, calmer, and more joyful. This transformation is the great work of the Guru. We must understand that the awakening of *kundalini* creates a revolution in our life, and this revolution is what we try to sum up in the word "purification."

Years ago I had a meditation vision in which Gurumayi handed me a glass that contained a red liquid, which she told me to drink. As soon as I swallowed the liquid, it created a tremendous upheaval inside me. A whirlwind of turbulence began to rise up from my lower abdomen. As it ascended through me, I had a sense that all kinds of debris had been kicked up and were flying around. Then, as it rose into my head, the tumult subsided and everything dissolved into a brilliant white light and a state of profound peace. Later, as I contemplated this experience, I understood that it symbolized my sadhana and the process of purification, initiated and supervised by the Guru.

Baba once said, "Remember that as long as your clogged mind has not been cleaned out, as long as your vessel has not been emptied and washed, you will not be able to fill it with God's nectar, nor will you be able to digest that nectar. It is important that your vessel be empty and completely purified in the fire of meditation and knowledge."[33]

Another aspect of this process is the purification of the senses. As *kundalinī* unfolds and we go deeper inside, the divine powers that reside in the senses are revealed. In other words, the senses become much more acute, sensitive, and strong. It is a matter of turning them around so they aren't always looking outside, but are able to see the inner worlds. We come across inner lights, we hear divine inner melodies and sounds, we smell inner fragrances and taste inner nectar. There is no adventure more marvelous. As the senses become pure, the mind becomes still. Meditation happens spontaneously.

But it is not as if the purifying and enlivening of our connection to our innermost Self deprives us of the ability to function in the world outside. On the contrary, the *shakti* that is awakened inside us also takes care of our outer life and improves it. Purification in Siddha Yoga meditation is not related to self-punishment, but to the freedom from whatever holds us back or holds us down. It is a process of lightening the accumulated weight of psychic and physical obstructions. The purification that happens inside us is reflected outwardly in the most auspicious way, and it manifests in a more generous, productive, and harmonious way of life. We are better able to live the way we really want to. Husbands and wives are able to express genuine affection and care for each other's well-being. Mothers and daughters stop fighting. Social relationships improve at home and in the workplace because they are no longer fraught with needs.

Baba explains it in this way: "As Kundalini works within us, She automatically transforms our outer life as well as our inner state. Our outlook changes, and we begin to see everything around us through new eyes. Relationships that may have seemed painful or dry become joyful and filled with affection. We feel an ever-expanding love for our family and friends, and gradually we start to see everyone around us as different forms of our own Self."[34]

This is the state of a Siddha — to see everyone as his own Self, that is to say, as divine. And that is exactly what starts to happen to us. However, this inner transformation requires effort and cooperation on our part. It's not as though we chant a few mantras or meditate for a few days and then a golden chariot descends to carry us to heaven. On several occasions in the past, when I was struggling with one negative tendency or another, I suddenly found Baba in his subtle form at my side. He showed me clear images of what my life would be like if I succumbed to those tendencies — it was a life of gray tones, delusion, pain, and despair. Then he showed me what my life would be like if I resisted and overcame those qualities. Light suddenly spread everywhere, and I was transported for a time into a higher, ecstatic state of expanded awareness. The choice was always mine. Over the years, the indelible memory of these experiences has given me courage and strength to face the challenges of the spiritual path.

Self-realization is the supreme goal of human life, and it is not acquired cheaply. Sadhana is sometimes called "the battle that must be fought." It is the great struggle between our higher and lower natures on the battlefield of our everyday life. In the Indian tradition, this is represented pictorially by the Goddess Durga astride a tiger, riding into battle against the demon hordes. The Goddess is the *shakti,* the great awakened energy, which slays the forces of darkness within us.

One of the things that can make the process of purification seem difficult at times is that we forget the nature of the force that is transforming us. The Guru is the *shakti* and is working within our lives at every moment. Baba constantly reminded us that the Guru is not just a person who wears nice clothes or hats, but the *shakti* that has been transmitted to us.

Along with the Guru's grace, Baba used to talk about the "disciple's grace." It is up to us to open ourselves to grace instead of pushing it away or resisting it. Devotion and faith draw grace toward us and sustain it. Sometimes this is not easy. The ego clings. Great chunks of our being oppose change. There are all kinds of hurdles and obstacles to be overcome. However, if we can nurture grace with a generous and humble heart and perform the spiritual practices given to us by the Guru in a dedicated manner, then real transformation can take place within us. The pace of purification is set somewhat by the disciple, by his ability to contemplate the teachings and look at his character, by the readiness with which he is able to see the play of his mind and ego, and most of all by the regularity and intensity with which he applies himself to the practices.

Gurumayi once said, "Even after you receive grace, you have to allow it to enter your life. Otherwise, grace is just waiting in the safe deposit box. You have to allow yourself to imbibe it; you have to allow yourself to cooperate with the workings of grace. . . .

"If you perform your practices truly, and continually ask for grace, then everything is protected, everything is respected, everything is taken care of."[35]

Some years ago, a man from Harlem in New York City said that he had grown up surrounded by crime and violence of every conceivable kind, and that his inner state was one of perpetual hatred and fear. One day he stumbled by accident, or so he thought, into a building that turned out to be the Siddha Yoga Meditation Ashram in Manhattan. He walked into the meditation hall and was powerfully drawn inward by the *shakti*. He sat down and immediately went into a state of deep meditation, in which he had an experience of the inner Self. Some time later, as he gradually came out of meditation, he realized that there was only one Being in the whole universe. An unknown love filled his heart — there was nobody to hate, for everyone and everything was a form of his own Self. Of course, at that point he wasn't able to sustain that state, but it changed his outlook forever.

One initial contact with the great Self is enough to change the direction of a person's life completely. The connection with the Self banishes bad feelings and violent tendencies. These deep inner experiences give us the conviction that allows us to engage in sadhana with a commitment that doesn't waver. But in order to expand this experience and make it stable, we have to allow the *shakti* to do its work, usually over a lengthy period of time.

Eventually, as a result of the process of purification, we begin to enter a state of intense, deep meditation that is beyond thought, beyond differences and duality. With the passing of time, we are able to stay there and come out of that state without losing its effects. At that point we don't see the people around us as antagonistic, hostile individuals. We see our own Self in everyone around us. Then the inner divine love is released and begins to pour through us. Tapping into this inner source of love is the hallmark of transformation.

In Baba's words, "Love is not something that is given or taken. If you think so, that is your wrong understanding. You have to make love well up inside yourself. Giving love and taking love are only outer forms; they are not the true nature of love. . . . Love surges within."[36]

The most potent aid to sadhana is love for the Guru. This draws the Guru's *shakti* in a way that nothing else can. When a disciple's love for the Guru is intense, the Guru appears to fill the entire world for him and he lives in a state of divine intoxication. This is a state that is hard for others to understand, but it holds the key to the state of union. Gurumayi once said, "God's love is ever present. God's love is in your heart, God's love is in my heart, and through this love we are connected forever."[37]

It is the simplest and most fundamental point of spiritual life, and yet it is perhaps the most difficult to grasp. The love that we feel for God and that fills the Guru connects us so surely and so utterly that at times all the barriers of individuality fall away and we discover we are living in the same Self. At times like these, we understand that there is no difference at all between the Guru and the disciple.

A few years ago, a woman was doing full-time seva, or selfless service, in the bakery of the Boston Ashram. At the end of the summer, she was invited to come spend the Labor Day weekend in South Fallsburg. When she arrived at Shree Muktananda Ashram, she went to the kitchen to offer her service, but she was totally preoccupied with one question — when and where would she have Gurumayi's darshan? She couldn't imagine returning to Boston without having seen her Guru. However, the situation was complicated by the fact that it was an Intensive weekend and Gurumayi would not be giving any other public programs. The woman knew she had to see Gurumayi — but how? Her yearning was so deep that her mind became completely one-pointed on the Guru. After spending a few hours doing seva in the kitchen, she became aware that she was seeing Gurumayi in everything — in the tomatoes, in the lettuce leaves, and in the other sevites. She could see the Guru pervading all forms.

Finally, when the Intensive let out in the late afternoon, she went in search of Gurumayi but wasn't able to find her, so she decided that the best thing to do was to continue to offer her service. She went to the bakery and found that Gurumayi had just arrived there. The woman scarcely dared to breathe as Gurumayi gave her a long look. "There you are!" Gurumayi said to her. "I was giving shaktipat to the people in the Intensive, but I only saw you. Everywhere I looked, there was only you. So I came looking for you. And, finally, here you are!" This is an extraordinary example, but it illustrates how the disciple's love and yearning draw the grace of the Guru, how they draw the Guru's *shakti* to oneself. Ultimately, that experience must take place entirely within.

The process of transformation is complete when the disciple merges into the Guru, when the light merges into the light forever. At its ultimate point, it is what Baba means when he says of his Guru, "It is his radiance in the light of my eyes. Through my breathing, it is he who comes in and goes out."[38] The disciple's being is totally realigned with the great Self. His system has been completely cleansed by the *shakti*, which can now flow through him unobstructed. His individuality is burned in the sacred fire of *kundalinī*, the fire of the Guru, and he attains divinity. The purpose of his life has been fulfilled.

If you have faith in the Guru's feet,
If you have deep feeling for the Guru's feet,
If you imbibe the state of the Guru,
Then you don't have to look for God.
God will come looking for you!

— Tukaram Maharaj

PART TWO

The GURU'S PĀDUKĀS

CHAPTER 1

THE HIDDEN MEANING
of the PĀDUKĀS

For a moment, clear your mind and imagine what early morning is like in Gurudev Siddha Peeth, an ashram nestled in the protection of a remote valley surrounded by sacred mountains in western India. The stillness of the *brahmamuhūrta*, the hours between 3:00 and 6:00 A.M., makes this time particularly favorable for spiritual practice. Night-blooming flowers fill the hushed courtyard with their fragrance. The solitary figures of devotees detach themselves from the shadows and move silently across the moonlit courtyard toward Swami Muktananda's Samadhi Shrine. It is the hour of meditation. As they enter one by one, they approach a carved marble pedestal on which a pair of silver *pādukās* rest. These sandals of the Guru, adorned with auspicious symbols and articles of worship — flowers, *kumkum*, sandalwood paste, and fragrant oils — reflect the gleaming light of the butter lamps placed on either side of them.

Each devotee pauses to rest his or her head on the sandals and offer a silent prayer. At that moment, some of them may experience something that is a great mystery: the sandals become luminous and transparent, and through them a subtle door opens into another realm, one that is beyond thoughts, where all divisive walls recede and shapes dissolve into pure Consciousness. The form has led to the Formless. This is the divine truth embodied by the Guru and concealed within the Guru's sandals.

An experience of this nature occurred for an Indian devotee of Baba Muktananda, when she welcomed a pair of his sandals into her house as if they were the living Guru himself. This was not a single experience, but one that expanded over quite a long period of time. She spoke about it with a depth of feeling and wonder that has only grown over the years. She said, "Two devotees arrived at my house holding a silver plate with Shri Baba's sandals, decorated with fragrant flowers. As soon as I saw those holy sandals, the force of the inner *shakti* increased a hundredfold, and for a moment I didn't understand what was happening to me. In a daze I ran for some flowers, offered them to the sandals, performed the *āratī*, and brought them into the house. Tears started streaming down my cheeks, and I began to do spontaneous *bhastrikā prānāyāma*, the 'bellows breathing.'

"I went into a state of deep meditation, and when I opened my eyes, everywhere I looked, I saw a bright blue effulgence. This continued for some time. I had experienced this same blue light once when I went into Baba's house in Ganeshpuri. The same effulgence, the same fragrance, and the same *shakti* of Baba's house filled our home when his sacred *pādukās* arrived. I heard Baba's voice speaking inside my head, saying,

'I have come to stay in your house. Don't worry. Everything will be all right.'

"The sandals are still in the meditation room in my home. When they arrived, all my worries began to disappear one by one. Now I enjoy the best of both worlds — spiritual and material.

"For the sake of the devotee, the formless Guru takes a form. My most venerable Guru lives in the sandals I worship. I carry out my duties and responsibilities with the understanding that my whole life is dedicated to my Guru. Baba sorts out all my problems; at a time when I was confronted with a mountain of suffering, he held my hand. All the members of my family experience that even a simple flower that has come in contact with Baba's sandals can work wonders.

"How can I ever forget my Guru's sandals? Every day I pray, 'O my Guru, wherever my mind goes, may your form be there. Wherever my head bows in salutation, may your feet be there.' "

The closer we come to the nature of the Guru, the more mysterious it seems. The embodiment of the Absolute, grace-bestowing power, giver of knowledge, purifier, remover of sorrow, conqueror of the obstacles that hold us back from the experience of our own true nature — all these, as we have seen, coalesce in the Guru. Having said this much, we are ready to approach the legendary representation of this mystery that resides in the Guru's feet or in the Guru's sandals, worshiped from the dawn of time.

Sculpted figures of the Guru's feet are among the earliest artifacts of Indian civilization. To this day, at every temple or *samādhi* shrine in India, a pair of sandals stand before the *mūrti*, the figure of the presiding deity of that place. Sometimes the sandals are wooden, sometimes ornately carved out of precious metals and adorned with gems. Mantras, ritual baths, elaborate ceremonies that have been scrupulously preserved for centuries and centuries are all dedicated to honoring, invoking, and worshiping the supreme power of the Absolute that resides in the Guru and, most especially, in the Guru's feet.

It is easy to understand the desire to worship the Guru, once we glimpse even for a moment the Guru's state and grace-bestowing power. But why the Guru's feet? Why not the Guru's face, the Guru's hands, or the Guru's eyes? Baba once said, "The Guru's feet are worshiped or revered because all the Guru's *shakti* dwells in the feet. If you did research into this with modern instruments, you would find that the vibrations of the inner Self constantly flow out through the feet. The nerves [of the subtle body] that come from the *sahasrāra* reach right down to the feet. The feet serve as the support for the whole body. This is the reason the feet are given so much importance. More *shakti* flows from the feet than from any other part of the body. The glory of the Guru's feet or the Guru's sandals is great."[1]

So the Guru's sandals are worshiped, just as the ground the Guru has walked on is worshiped, and great reverence is given to the dust under the Guru's feet. The *shakti* that flows through them makes them all instruments of shaktipat, of divine initiation, and the grace of God. This is why the sacred texts glorify the Guru's sandals and tell of the miracles they accomplish. For example, the *Kulārnava Tantra* says: "Remember the Guru's sandals. . . . They provide protection against great diseases, great disturbances, great evils, great fears, great calamities, and great sins."[2]

The seminal event in the modern history of Siddha Yoga meditation, the fountainhead from which this great outpouring of grace streamed through the world, is the initiation that Baba Muktananda was given by his Guru, Bhagawan Nityananda. From that awakening came the initiation of thousands. When we hear the story of Baba's shaktipat, which he tells so beautifully in *Play of Consciousness*, his spiritual autobiography, we can almost feel the hand of Bhagawan Nityananda reaching into the future. The act of initiation itself was invisible, of course, but Bhagawan Nityananda also gave Baba something tangible to carry away with him, as if to mark with these sacred objects the immense transition into greatness that had just been conferred upon him.

Baba writes:

> Bhagawan Nityananda said, "Take these sandals, put them on." Then he asked, "You'll wear my sandals?" I was amazed, but replied reverently and firmly, "Gurudev, these sandals are not to be worn by my feet. Babaji, they are for me to worship all my life. I'll spread my shawl, and then please be so gracious as to put your feet on it and leave your sandals there."
>
> Gurudev agreed. . . . He lifted his left foot, and its sandal, and placed it on the edge of my outspread shawl. Then he put his foot down, raised his right

foot, and placed the other sandal on the shawl. . . .

My Gurudev was a great *avadhūta*. He would wander through the world barefooted, never wearing sandals. But today he had worn sandals on his lotus feet, those feet which bestow the knowledge of yoga, which destroy our sins and are adored by gods and men. He had walked around, come before me, and raising his lotus feet, given me his sandals. My anguish had been lifted from me, my sins cut away, the cycle of birth and death ended, the curtain of ignorance removed.[3]

This action and the beautiful way Baba honors it give us some insight into the immense power of grace, knowledge, and transformation embodied in the Guru's sandals. As Baba says, the Guru's sandals bestow the knowledge of yoga: they open the way to the most sublime spiritual realities. They actuate purification and destroy sins. Contact with them tears the fabric of the false mental world we have so elaborately constructed, and a divine force breaks through into our everyday lives. What we thought was solid turns out to be ephemeral, as arbitrary and evanescent as the mist that rises off a lake in the morning, and we see through it to the real ground of our being and our lives. What we considered concrete and real is actually nothing but the haze of ignorance issuing from the limited ego, made of opinions and concepts all blurry and running together. The Guru's sandals lift us beyond the anguish caused by all this duality and multiplicity. Ultimately, they are the vehicle through which the individual soul merges into God, putting an end to the cycle of birth and death.

The experience that Baba Muktananda described in his spiritual autobiography echoes through the consciousness of future devotees, whether they are aware of the language and figures associated with the Indian tradition or not. For instance, a woman taking an Intensive with Gurumayi in South Fallsburg, New York, closed her eyes for meditation and received initiation in the most classical fashion in a vision, which she described like this: "Gurumayi stretched out both her feet, and a beautiful and strong current of fire burst from her feet and entered my being through my mouth as I was chanting *Om*. I felt a sweet river of love rushing through my soul." There are many similar descriptions from people who had never previously known of the significance of the Guru's feet.

Eastern spiritual traditions have always taken into account the subtle body of a human being. This subtle body is an energy body interpenetrating the physical body, and it is composed of millions of tiny conduits, meridians, or *nādīs*, that form an intricate web carrying the *prāna*, or vital force, throughout the system.

According to Chinese medicine, for instance, the body contains many acupuncture meridians, or channels, which all congregate around the feet. At a therapeutic level, specific areas of the feet correspond to many of the internal organs. By treating the feet, the Chinese physician adjusts the flow of energy along the channels to the different organs and parts of the body. Additionally, there is a particular acupuncture point in the sole of the foot called *yongquan*, which is translated into English as "gushing spring." When a person needs energy, he is taught to focus his mind on this point. Sooner or later there is an energy charge that goes from the mind to this point in the sole of the foot, and from there energy shoots up to the crown of the head. It is a major point for both meditation and acupuncture in the Chinese tradition.

In the case of a Siddha, a perfected Master whose system has been completely cleansed of impurities and blockages by the awakened *kundalinī*, all the channels or *nādīs* are clear and the currents of *shakti* can flow unimpeded and with great force, particularly through the feet.

In the early 1970s in the Ganeshpuri Ashram, there was not yet a clinic or an ample first-aid station to treat ashramites who got bitten by the occasional scorpion while walking along the lush garden paths. I remember several instances when we would hear people shrieking for help, unable to walk. Baba would come out of his house, hurry to the garden, and touch the area of the bite with his foot. The person would immediately calm down, get up, and walk away without pain.

However healing they may be, Baba always cautioned us not to confuse the Guru's feet with the physical limbs. He emphasized again and again that the Guru is not a human being; the Guru is a cosmic force functioning through a human body. At one point he said, "The Guru's feet refer to the Being in whom the Guru stands rooted, and that Being is the supreme Being, that Being is the highest Truth. . . . The lotus feet of the Guru are the most sacred centers for a disciple. They encompass all sacred centers. If a disciple worships this sacred place, he worships all sacred places."[4]

The Guru is said to be the place of all pilgrimage because the Absolute resides in him. We find in the living Guru the divine Presence that people go to temples to invoke. Therefore, by worshiping at the feet of the Guru, one worships holiness itself. Over and over again, however, the living Master will guide the disciple's attention away from the physical form of the Guru's feet on the outside to the ones that reside at the crown of the disciple's own head. This is the crux of the mystery of the Guru and the Guru's feet: they are both within and without.

CHAPTER 2

HAMSA *or* SO'HAM

In Sanskrit, the word *pāda* means "foot." It also means "place, position, or station." Baba said, "The Guru's feet are like the foundation on which a building stands. . . . The Guru's feet are the two elements in the mantra *So'ham*, which means 'I am That.'"[5]

The Guru's feet represent that inner place where we come to stand firmly in the knowledge of our true identity, our oneness with the vast ocean of Consciousness deep within us. When we reach the feet of the Guru inside us, we reach God.

During an Intensive, a woman had the following experience. She said, "I began repeating the mantra on my inhalations and exhalations. Suddenly the mantra grew so powerful and the vibration was so fierce that I was afraid and could hardly repeat it. But I kept on. Next, my breathing began to get very irregular; my body was forgetting how to breathe. I felt as if I was going to strangle. Then I heard Gurumayi say, 'Just leave your thoughts on the shore.' I knew she was the ocean and my body was the shore.

"My breath almost stopped. It was very irregular and gasping. Suddenly I saw Gurumayi in front of me, holding out her arms, standing in the ocean of Consciousness. She said, 'Don't be afraid to drown.' I still struggled for breath until, a second later, a breath filled me — not my breath, but the breath of God. I felt like a newborn baby taking its first breath. The breath went out completely, then came back in. My body was being breathed by God — each breath. I understood that I am a pulsation of that ocean of Consciousness.

"I realized that *ham* and *sa* were reversed, that it is truly *So'ham*. My inhalation is God's exhalation and my exhalation is God's inhalation, and that ocean of Consciousness is what is real. When this body exhales for the last time, it will only be the inhalation of that one Consciousness that has no beginning and no end, which is Gurumayi, Baba, and Bhagawan Nityananda — the eternal One. That ocean of Consciousness knows no death.

"The breath was so clear, so free. There was so much ecstasy, the bliss of Consciousness. It was not this body breathing, but the ocean of Consciousness pulsing and maintaining this body. Each breath was absolute bliss."

The statement *So'ham*, "That I am," or *Hamsa*, "I am That," is so rich in meaning that it has to be unpacked if we are to appreciate and understand it fully. Actually, the best way to understand it is to experience each layer of its meaning in meditation. Once we have received shaktipat, we can begin to access the essence of *So'ham* or *Hamsa* because it lives within us as a reality. So an interesting way to approach the material that we are about to explore is as a series of aids to our practice of meditation. Everything that follows is called into play when the meditator repeats *So'ham*. Lalleshwari, a wandering saint of Kashmir, wrote luminous poetry in the everyday language of ordinary people. Once she said:

> As long as I failed
> to see my Self,
> I could not see the ocean
> even though I was drowning.
> When I held aloft the torch of *So'ham*,
> I saw that I was the ocean itself.[6]

These two syllables, *ham* and *sa*, have a number of esoteric meanings. Let's examine what they are. *Ham* is Shiva, the all-pervasive supreme Reality, the absolute Being. He is the Lord or God, the support and foundation of all things, sentient and insentient. In the form of pure Consciousness, He permeates all creatures and dwells in them as their own innermost Self. He is the still center of our being, the true "I," the experiencing subject. The scriptures also call this experiencer the *purusha*, the eternal Witness.

Sa is Shakti, the energy of Shiva. As we have seen, Shakti is the divine cosmic power that creates and maintains the countless galaxies and worlds. She is the consort of Shiva, the active aspect of the formless, attributeless Absolute. She is the joyous divine energy that unfolds the universe, assuming the billions of shapes and forms that we see around us. Whereas Shiva is the experiencer, Shakti is what is experienced, the objective universe. She is also referred to as *prakriti*, or the force of nature. Within us, She is the energy that powers our mind and that enables us to walk, talk, eat our meals, and perform our work.

The *Guru Gītā* says that the Guru's feet have two different lusters — one is white and the other is red — representing Shiva and Shakti.[7] Shiva is associated with the color white, and Shakti, the divine energy, with the color red.

On this subject Baba says:

> In these feet Shiva and Shakti live as one, and through them the disciple realizes that unity. He sees Shiva and Shakti as red and white lights shining through the Guru's feet. The Guru's feet should be worshiped every day, for by their means one easily realizes the immanent and transcendent aspects of Shiva. Their luster radiates in the upper spaces of the *sahasrāra*. Accessible and inaccessible to speech, mind, and imagination; shining white and red, red and white are the Guru's feet. Muktananda, worship them always.[8]

By worshiping the Guru's feet, Shiva can be realized in His immanent aspect, in which He pervades the material world as the subtle light suffusing all seemingly substantial forms. In this immanent aspect, He is accessible to speech, mind, and imagination. Worshiping the Guru's feet can also lead to the direct perception of Shiva's transcendent aspect, that which is beyond name and form, and which no word or thought can approach.

CHAPTER 3

BINDU *and* VISARGA

Now that we have briefly examined *ham* and *sa* as Shiva and Shakti, Consciousness and its energy, we can move on to another level of meaning. *Ham* is also considered to be the *bindu*, and *sa* is defined as *visarga*.[9] In Sanskrit grammar, the *bindu* is a dot that is placed above a letter to give it a nasal resonance. *Visarga* consists of two dots written one above the other like a colon [:] at the end of a word. *Visarga* gives the word a final aspiration, the sound of "h," which entails the expulsion of the breath.

On the cosmic level, *ham*, the *bindu*, is the dimensionless point into which the universe is absorbed, the subsiding back into formlessness, into Shiva. *Sa, visarga*, is emanation or creation, the issuing forth of Shakti into manifestation and form. Similarly, on the individual level, *ham*, or the *bindu*, represents the in-breath, the still point into which all thoughts and perceptions are absorbed. *Sa*, or *visarga*, is the outgoing breath, the creation of the world of perceptions, thoughts, and ideas. The word *Hamsa*, then, represents the union of these two opposites, of male and female, Shiva and Shakti, the world within and the world without.

Baba once said, "God lives within us in the form of *Hamsa*." In that statement he is referring to *Hamsa* or *So'ham* as mantra. It is called the natural mantra because it repeats itself spontaneously within us whether we are aware of it or not. *So'ham* is the sound of our breath. It is what gives us life and it is God. This natural, self-repeating mantra is built into our very system. Not only that, it is *So'ham* that forms the two feet of the Guru within us.

This is an astonishing fact — our breath is mantra, and the resonance of these sacred syllables that are both God and Goddess is the etheric substance out of which the feet of the Guru in the crown of our head are formed. They are made of breath, they are made of sound, they are made of mantra, and the mantra signifies the highest truth — "I am That, I am the Absolute." So, when the *Guru Gītā* says, "The root of worship is the Guru's feet,"[10] we begin to see what lies behind such a statement — the highest teachings, the highest Reality, condensed into this single, nectarean, grace-bestowing form.

Let's look a bit deeper. The mantra *So'ham* goes on constantly inside us, as we have just said. We watch the breath with the awareness that it is coming in and going out with these two sacred syllables. We witness the unending dance of Shiva and Shakti, of God and His energy, going on within us as it does within the world. As these syllables dissolve on the inside and on the outside, for a split second there is no thought, no feeling, nothing. Then from this moment of nothingness the syllables arise once again.

It is in this space where there is neither thought nor feeling that the Truth exists. Boundaries dissolve, and the outside and the inside become one. These syllables are so powerful that becoming aware of them draws us deep into meditation, and ultimately into that high state where the darshan of the Guru's feet becomes accessible to us.

As long as we perceive the world and ourselves through the blinders of duality, as long as we feel that we are different, separate from others, and that we are limited and small, we cannot experience true happiness. The sense that there is someone other than ourselves is the source of all fear and suffering. However, when we are able to maintain the awareness of *Hamsa* or *So'ham*, "I am That," we draw near to the inner reality of the Guru's feet, the profound state of absolute union and equality-consciousness in which the Guru is established.

Jnaneshwar Maharaj said, "Just as light pervades everywhere, the *So'ham* consciousness extends from the embodied Self to the supreme Self. When man becomes fully immersed in the vision of *So'ham*, he spontaneously merges in the supreme Being."[11]

This final merging into the Absolute is the crowning glory of the path of *bhakti*, devotion. *Bhakti*, as the Gurus of our lineage point out, is an inner attitude of the heart that expresses itself outwardly in the form of worship. Here we are at the peak of the sacred paradox we call the Guru. This is a mystery that sincere devotees on the path experience at one time or another, sooner or later: when we approach the physical feet of the Guru with an attitude of worship, when our inner being is ripe for the experience, then these feet reveal their transcendent aspect and draw us like a magnet into the great heart of Consciousness within us.

Gurumayi once said, "The feet of the Guru, *So'ham*, are the source of liberation. When your mind becomes absorbed in this awareness, *So'ham*, 'I am That,' you shed your false sense of separation and limitation. Your mind becomes very pure. This is why the Guru's feet are worshiped — to absorb the mind in the experience of *So'ham*."[12]

The Indian tradition often refers to the individual soul with the word *Hamsa*. Another meaning for the same word in Sanskrit is "swan," which is why we frequently find the soul represented as a swan. The scriptures and esoteric texts that speak of *kundalinī* locate the individual soul in the heart chakra, *anāhata*, in the region of the chest. The *paramahamsa*, supreme swan, is the universal Soul, pure Consciousness, God. It is said by these scriptures to be seated in the *sahasrāra*, the highest spiritual center at the crown of the head.

Even though this may sound abstruse, it is something that is experienced by many practitioners of Siddha Yoga meditation. For instance, here is a story that I heard just a few months ago. A woman who was staying in Shree Muktananda Ashram in South Fallsburg, New York, and who was unaware of all the explanations above, said that one morning when she sat for meditation, she saw a beautiful swan inside her, beating its wings vigorously, taking off in flight. It soared and soared, and as the woman watched, she asked it, "Where are you going? What is your final destination?" Just then, a humming sound began in the upper part of her head. Suddenly, she saw the Guru's *pādukās* in the crown of her own head, and she realized that the humming sound was the vibration emanating from these sandals. At that point, the swan descended and lay down over the *pādukās*, and the music of *So'ham-Hamsa* began to resound within her. She understood that this is the final destination, the awareness of *So'ham*, "I am That."

If the Guru's feet are within us, how and where do we meditate on them? There is a beautiful short Sanskrit text of seven verses called the *Pāduka Pañchaka*.[13] This hymn is attributed to Lord Shiva; that is to say, it is considered a revealed text. It describes in great detail the Guru's feet inside us, where they are situated, what they look like, how to visualize them for worship, and how to meditate on them. By meditating on the Guru's feet, we are led to the ultimate goal, merging with the Guru, letting our narrow, limited notions of ourselves dissolve in the supreme mystery of the Guru's all-encompassing state.

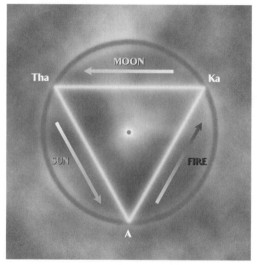

A-Ka-Tha Triangle

CHAPTER 4

A-KA-THA TRIANGLE

～

The *Pādukā Pañchaka* speaks of two lotuses, or spiritual centers: the *sahasrāra*, the brilliant white lotus of a thousand petals that is located at the crown of the head, and also a smaller twelve-petaled lotus that is situated within the pericarp, or center, of the *sahasrāra*. Imagine, for a moment, two white lotuses, one above the other, with their centers touching. The *sahasrāra* is the large upper lotus, which is downward-turned, and the smaller twelve-petaled lotus is beneath it and upward-turned. These lotuses are extremely subtle; they are not made of solid substance but of light, visible only to the subtle eye.

In the center where these lotuses meet, there is a triangle with its apex pointing down. The lines of this triangle are actually composed of all the letters of the Sanskrit alphabet; so it might be said that the Guru's feet, which are within this triangle, sit inside the source of all language and sound. This triangle is called *a-ka-tha*, after the letters that stand at the beginning of its three lines. *A* and the sixteen Sanskrit vowels that follow it start at the downward-pointing apex of this triangle and extend up the right side. The first sixteen consonants beginning with *ka* form the second line, extending across the top of the triangle from right to left. The second sixteen consonants beginning with *tha* form the third line, extending down the left side of the triangle back to the apex. The three remaining Sanskrit letters, *ha, lla,* and *ksha,* are located inside the angles of this *a-ka-tha* triangle.

From this place, the highest seat in the subtle body, all these letters then come down through the chakras in a certain sequence. We can imagine them descending from the *a-ka-tha* triangle through the rest of the subtle body. Each letter has its own place on a certain petal in a certain chakra in our system.[14]

There are other elements contained in the *a-ka-tha* triangle. The sun, moon, and fire are images that appear frequently in the texts that speak of *kundalinī.* These are forms the great light takes when it descends into the realm of matter. The lines of this triangle represent these three images of light, as well as the *trimūrti,* or trinity, of the Indian tradition: Brahma, Vishnu, and Shiva. The lines are also connected with the three *gunas,* or qualities of nature: *sattva,* goodness and purity; *rajas,* passion and activity; and *tamas,* darkness and inertia. The first line of the *a-ka-tha* triangle is the line of fire, and since the sacred texts associate fire with the origin of life, this line is connected with Brahma, the Creator, and *rajoguna.* The second line of the triangle is the line of the moon. Its coolness and purity are associated with Vishnu, the Preserver, and with *sattvaguna.* The third line of the triangle is the line of the sun, representing the twelve suns that rise to burn the world at the time of dissolution; so it is connected with Shiva in his form as Rudra, the Destroyer, and with *tamoguna*. The sacred texts often call the *sahasrāra* the region of sun, moon, and fire, and it is this triangle to which they are referring.

At the very center of the *a-ka-tha* triangle is the supreme *bindu*, or Blue Pearl. It is a small, brilliant blue dot the size of a sesame seed, yet it is the source of everything. The *bindu* is the first form to emerge out of *mahāshūnya*, the Great Void. *Mahāshūnya* is emptiness in the sense that it is without manifest creation, and yet it is filled with the potential of all conceivable names, forms, and worlds. The *bindu* is the state of the gathered-up power of Consciousness that is about to create the universe. Therefore, it is called the "primordial seed of the universe," or the "cosmic creative drop." All of the combined energies of creation — from lightning bolts and raging rivers to the subtlest radiance of God — lie in a potential form within the Blue Pearl. The *bindu* is also luminous: it is not only a drop of energy but of subtle light.

Speaking about this supreme *bindu*, Baba says:

> In the light of the blue jewel
> the poor become rich and the joyless joyful.
> The ignorant are filled with knowledge
> and virtue grows where before there was none.

> Those who see the Blue Pearl,
> the light blazing through *sahasrāra's* sun,
> are the most blessed.

> The rising of yogic realization,
> the setting of the illusion of the world,
> the attainment of the state of wisdom
> are all caused by the glowing Blue Pearl. [15]

When we read these descriptions of the inner world by the great beings, it is marvelous, almost startling, to remember that all this is right inside us, as well.

In meditation, a woman saw very clearly the blue sphere of the universe with the Guru's sandals in the center. Then it seemed that every particle of the universe contained the blue sphere with the Guru's sandals in the center. It was like a hologram: each part contained the whole. Every particle of the universe contained the power of grace, Self-knowledge, unity-awareness. She felt that every cell of her body was a blue sphere with the Guru's sandals in the center. Then she became aware of her whole body as huge, as Shiva, the one Consciousness. For days, that awareness of the blue sphere remained with her as she walked around.

The Blue Pearl is the seat of *turīya*, the fourth or transcendental state of consciousness, beyond the three commonly experienced states of waking, dreaming, and deep sleep. *Turīya* is the state in which a great being becomes established after enlightenment — it is unbreakable, unwavering beatitude and bliss. The Blue Pearl and *turīya* are associated with the supracausal body, whose seat is the *sahasrāra*. The state of deep sleep is experienced in the causal body, located in the heart. The dream state corresponds to the subtle body, seated in the throat; and the waking state is experienced in the physical body, whose seat is in the eyes.[16]

It is said that this supreme *bindu* germinates and sprouts into three other Pearls or *bindus*, which mark the angles of the *a-ka-tha* triangle. This primordial triangle is also known as the cosmic womb that gives birth to all the sounds represented by the letters of the alphabet, as we have seen. According to the tradition of Kashmir Shaivism, the universe is born from subtle sound vibration.[17] It is in fact nothing but a solidification of this vibration. In other words, the universe is born from the Blue Pearl.

The *Guru Gītā* speaks of this triangle, saying, "In the round space of the thousand-petaled lotus, there is a triangular lotus, which is formed by the three lines beginning with *a*, *ka*, and *tha*, and which has *ham* and *sah* on two sides. One should remember the Guru, who is seated in its center."[18]

The *Pādukā Pañchaka* says that the *a-ka-tha* triangle has the character of a mandala. A mandala, as we usually understand it, is a diagram which is ritualistically created as an act of worship of a particular deity. The object of worship is summoned and appears in the form of the mandala. So just as it is said that mantra is the sound body of a deity, a mandala, or *yantra*, is a deity in the form of color and geometric design. However, the *a-ka-tha* triangle inside our own head is a mandala which is naturally formed — that is, self-created — and in it are set the feet of the Guru. When a seeker meditates on the Guru's feet, it is here that they are envisioned. This object of worship is not just built into us; it is from this place that our very being has evolved.

Sometimes people think that these experiences are so exalted that they are beyond reach. They assume that they can't hope to experience these things until they have done thirty or forty years of sadhana. But with grace, anything is possible. These experiences are gifts of the Guru's grace and can come at any time.

There was a woman who was completely new to Siddha Yoga meditation and who was meditating at an introductory program given by one of the swamis. After she had been repeating the mantra for about ten minutes, she became aware of an intense sensation of heat in the back of her neck. As it moved upward, she saw the stalk of a flower, crowned with many petals, rising up to the top of her head. In the midst of the petals a triangle appeared, which later turned into the figure of a yogi seated in meditation. Several days later, when she was looking through a copy of *Play of Consciousness*, she recognized the photo of Bhagawan Nityananda, Baba's Guru, as the yogi who had appeared inside her in her meditation. She had no idea of the significance of any of this at the time; but the more her knowledge of Siddha Yoga meditation philosophy grew, the more this indelible image resonated with meaning. This is one of the defining characteristics of a spiritual experience. However fleeting the actual vision may be, its sense and relevance and depth of meaning continue to unfold for years. Not only that, to invoke it is to reexperience it.

The *Pādukā Pañchaka* tells us that as we visualize the place of the Guru within the triangle at the crown of the head, we are to "meditate on the primordial *Hamsa*, the all-powerful great light in which the universe is absorbed."[19] So when we meditate on

Hamsa here, it is with the awareness, "I am That," the awareness of merging into the great light that is the supreme Guru.

CHAPTER 5

THE LOTUS

The *Pādukā Pañchaka* continues: "The mind there contemplates the two lotuses which are the feet of the Guru, and of which the ruby-colored nectar is the honey. These two feet are cool like the nectar of the moon, and are the place of all auspiciousness."[20]

Once again, this is a metaphor referring to a sublime yogic experience. Let's examine these images more closely. Very often, as we have seen, they condense a great deal of meaning into a deceptively simple image.

For example, why does the lotus symbolize the sacred? Although it grows from the muddy floor of a lake, the lotus flower is pure and unsoiled and, therefore, exemplifies how one should live in the world. The lotus is also a symbol of *shakti* and represents the unfolding of power, or the divine essence. While it is still a bud, it marks the stage of approach to the realization of the great Self. When the blazing sun of Consciousness shines upon it, the bud opens to the fullness and the perfection of its potential. In the iconography of the Eastern religions, many deities are depicted as seated on a lotus throne or as standing on a lotus. These images symbolize both purity and spiritual authority.

The lotus is also a frequent image in *kundalinī yoga*. The chakras are spiritual centers strung along the *sushumnā nādī*, the central channel of the subtle body that corresponds to the spinal column in the physical body. These centers of subtle energy are often described as lotuses with varying numbers of petals. The petals are formed by the configurations of the *nādīs*, which surround and pass through the chakras. The petals of the lotuses hang downward, except when the awakened *kundalinī* rises through them. As the *nādīs* are filled with the radiant *shakti*, the lotuses appear to turn upward and bloom with light. So this one simple image, the lotus, is rich with meaning and auspicious implications. It is intimately associated with the experience of God.

CHAPTER 6

N E C T A R

~

We have seen that the *a-ka-tha* triangle is situated in the center where two lotuses meet — the *sahasrāra* and the smaller, twelve-petaled lotus. Now, this image is enriched by an additional image — another natural, self-formed mandala, the full moon, inside which the *a-ka-tha* triangle and the feet of the Guru rest. Within the mandala of the moon in the *sahasrāra* can be found the mysterious "pot of nectar" of which the poet-saints and mystics speak, and which is often referred to as "the nectar of the moon." This pot of nectar has the shape of a delicate crescent moon and is downward-turned. From here, nectar flows down through the *sushumnā nāḍī*. This nectar is always described in the scriptures as being of a ruby red color. The verse we quoted above compares it to honey because of its taste, which is sweet but not sticky, as it drops onto the palate. However, it is more intoxicating than any honey ever could be. Baba says: "The sound [the inner *nāda* heard in meditation] will make you taste a divine elixir. The elixir released by this sound drops from the palate and is very beautiful. It is sweeter than the sweetest. Each drop is worth millions. It is worthy of being treasured by everyone.

By taking it you get rid of all sickness. As you taste it, you will be filled with joy, and afterward you will find that taste in whatever you eat or drink, whether it is cooked or uncooked, simple or dry. There will be no more suffering, no more want, no more feeling of 'I and mine.' You yourself will become the vessel of this elixir, and subsequently you will find the elixir of love in your husband, your wife, and your children. . . . This is the essence of the gods, the essence of love, the essence of yoga, and the essence you have been searching for in the world."[21]

A woman who was staying in Shree Muktananda Ashram said that one morning at 4:00 as she sat for meditation, a giant ball of energy suddenly started vibrating in the pit of her abdomen. It began making a thunderous roar and pulsating so heavily that she became afraid. Then it began to surge up through her body. But as it went through her stomach up toward her chest, she lost her fear, because in its wake it was leaving ecstasy. As the energy began to surge through her neck, through her head, and burst out of the crown of her head, it showered a sweet nectar over her. Her entire being, from the outside in, became ecstatic. She went into meditation, and when she came out, that ecstatic feeling stayed with her the whole day, the whole night, until the next morning. After that she felt she was a different person. She knew that she had experienced the truth of what Gurumayi and Baba have said over and over again, "God dwells within you as you." That experience, that power, and that nectar were awesome to her. She knew, through the Guru's grace, that she wasn't just a human being, she was also divine.

The *Lalitā Sahasranāma* says: "Salutations to Her [Shakti] who sends streams of nectar from the transcendent moon in the *sahasrāra*."[22]

And the *Shiva Samhitā* says: "The *sahasrāra* is the thousand-petaled lotus in the *brahmarandhra*. In its center is the region of the moon and a triangle which continually showers nectar. This moon nectar, which grants immortality, flows in a continuous stream. . . ."[23]

Once when Baba was visiting New Delhi, I overheard a woman complaining to him, saying, "My daughter gets floods of nectar every time she sits for meditation, but I get only a trickle." Baba laughed and replied that a trickle of that divine nectar was more than enough and was a great blessing, indeed!

The *Pādukā Pañchaka* also mentions that the Guru's feet are cool like the nectar of the moon. In other words, just as moonbeams cool us off after the heat of the day, in the same way devotion to the feet of the Guru extinguishes the fire of sorrow and suffering and gives us peace.

Verse 6 of the *Pādukā Pañchaka* says: "I adore the two lotus feet of the Guru in my head. The jeweled footstool on which they rest removes all sin. The Guru's feet are pinkish-red like young leaves. The toenails resemble the full moon shining in all its glory. The Guru's feet are radiant with the beautiful luster of lotuses growing in a lake of nectar."

When the *Guru Gītā* speaks of the water of the Guru's feet, it is referring to this same lake of nectar.

There are a number of verses that explore this image. For instance, verse 13 of the *Guru Gītā* says, "The water of the Guru's feet has the power to dry up the mire of one's sins, to ignite the light of knowledge, and to take one smoothly across the ocean of this world."

And verse 14 continues: "To obtain knowledge and detachment, sip the water of the Guru's feet, which destroys ignorance and ends karmas, the cause of rebirth."

In other words, when our spiritual practices have evolved to such a high degree that our awareness enters the *sahasrāra* and the nectar in that center begins to stream through our being, then the ties of worldly ignorance that bind us let go. Baba Muktananda's elucidation of these esoteric mysteries is very clear. Baba says: "It is not the water of the Guru's physical feet that will make you immortal; it is only the nectar flowing in the Guru's abode situated in the *sahasrāra* that will make you immortal, and that nectar can be received by the grace of the Guru.

"In the course of your meditation, when the mind becomes stabilized in the *sahasrāra*, this nectar begins to flow. Only after drinking this nectar can you be said to have drunk the water of the Guru's feet. . . . It is not the water of the Guru's physical feet that matters. The true feet of the Guru lie in the *sahasrāra*; it is the nectar flowing from them that gives immortality. A meditator can gain access to this nectar only through meditation, only through the grace of the Guru."[24]

We have attempted to examine some of the rich images associated with the Guru's feet and sandals and to decipher what they mean in terms of the actual inner yogic experiences that come to us as a result of the Guru's grace. These experiences reach their culmination when at last we merge with the Guru's feet. At that time, we leave behind the realm of names and forms, and cross over the threshold to the Formless, the Supreme.

One man tells us of a powerful and vivid dream that he had during the first three months that he spent with Baba. He says: "In this dream I approached a door, opened the door, and saw Baba sitting inside. He wasn't sitting in a room. There were no walls, no ceiling, no floor. It was as though he was perched in space.

"When I saw him, something burst forth in my heart unlike anything I had ever experienced or imagined. It was a wrenching sensation, as if I had just found that which I had yearned for all my life. I literally ran to him, crying. . . . As I neared him, I dove at his feet, and he simultaneously stretched his legs out toward me, as though enabling me to get to his feet more easily. He was laughing and saying things in a language I didn't understand. It didn't seem to matter what he said. The meaning was clear.

"I took his feet in my hands as I did a full *pranām*, and pressed his feet against the top of my head. Then I experienced that my head and his feet merged into each other. With Baba's feet on my head, I became one with him and experienced myself as the center of the universe, like some central sun of pure light and being, which emanated the entire cosmos from its own Self.

"This sublime experience seemed to last awhile, and then I woke up feeling permeated by the brightest light I had ever known. Even though it was dark outside, the entire room was filled with effulgence. The brilliance of the light and the intensity of the *shakti* pulsating within me made it impossible for me to return to sleep that night. I remained in waking meditation, and the entire next day I was filled with light and boundless energy."[25]

Baba once said, "An unwavering *bhakta* (devotee) always longs for the ever-fresh and pure love of his Guru. No other desire remains in his heart. . . . In short, his only longing is for the lotus feet of the *sadguru*.

"When such a rare longing arises by Shri Gurudev's grace, the devotee, taking full advantage of this state of blissfulness that even the sages crave, becomes free from the cycle of birth and death. His heart then becomes Gurudev's temple. The union between an ardent devotee and the beloved Guru is in itself immortality. This culmination is the height of *gurubhakti*."[26]

Once a devotee savors the bliss of union with the Guru, there is no longer any question of conquering the senses or of trying to still the turbulent mind. The raging current of the river reaches the ocean and comes to rest forever. That ocean is the Guru.

"The significance of the Guru cannot be understood by one who is not a disciple," Baba once said. "The Guru's greatness defies all words."[27] In place of a thousand definitions, explanations, hymns, and songs of glory, the Indian tradition offers us the mystery of an image — the Guru's sandals. Attainable only when the accumulated merits of hundreds of lifetimes bring us in contact with a true Guru in his physical form, the feet of the Guru at the crown of the head still guide us and beckon to us. We are That. Even after the awakening of *kundalini*, which brings the supreme goal of human existence into our range, even then, a disciple has years and years of spiritual practice ahead of him. His journey accelerates, yes, but the path is arduous, and narrow are the gates. It is the Guru and the Guru's sandals that sustain, protect, and inspire a disciple within and without, all along the way. They are an inexhaustible source of comfort and guidance, a defense against all dangers. As such, they have been worshiped and revered for thousands of years.

One of the most beautiful examples of this is contained in the *Rāmāyana*. It tells the story of Bharata, the younger brother of Lord Rama, who refused to accept the kingdom of Ayodhya during Rama's exile in the forest, because his own mother's ambition for him had been the cause of Rama's banishment. Bharata went to the forest in search of Rama, hoping to perform the coronation ceremony for him there and afterward to bring him home to the palace. But Rama, faithful to the laws of dharma, would not break his promise to go into exile and declined to accompany Bharata back to Ayodhya. Bharata hunted out a pair of costly sandals and said, "Here are sandals inlaid with gold. I beg you to stand on them for a moment. Blessed by the touch of your holy feet, these sandals will become sanctified, and they will bear the burden of ruling the kingdom."

Rama smiled at Bharata and stood for a moment wearing the golden sandals. Then he gave them back to his brother. Bharata prostrated before the sandals and said, "My beloved brother, I will dress like a renunciant in coarse tree bark and deerskin, and will wear matted locks until your term of exile is over in fourteen years. I will wait for you to come back, and I will live outside the city of Ayodhya, in Nandigrama. I will place these sandals on the throne, and they will rule the kingdom as your symbols. I will merely serve as your representative."

Bharata took the sandals in his hands, placed them with reverence on his head, and did *pradakshina*, walking clockwise around Rama three times. Still carrying the *pādukās* on his head, Bharata ascended his chariot. Eventually he reached Nandigrama, where the coronation of the *pādukās* would take place.

Bharata addressed the elders and said, "I have been appointed guardian of the country by my revered brother. His sandals will rule the kingdom." He bowed to the sandals and spoke again: "To me, these are the blessed feet of my brother. The white umbrella indicating royalty will be held above them, and they will inspire me to walk on the right path and never to swerve from it. I will guard them with my life. One day, I will see them adorning my brother's feet, and I will find peace of mind."

Dressed in tree bark and deerskin, Bharata lived outside of Ayodhya. He would speak to the sandals and report to them about the various happenings in the kingdom as though they were human. He did nothing without consulting them. And they, in turn, granted him the insight and wisdom he needed to resolve every situation in a just and righteous manner. Dedicating everything to the *pādukās*, Bharata ruled the kingdom for fourteen years, until Rama returned victorious from the forest, having defeated the mighty demon Ravana.

~

Before final realization, when the longed-for experience of God in every moment is something we cannot yet sustain, when we long for God and union with the Guru as Bharata longed for Rama, then we — like this noble brother — invoke the wisdom and love, the solutions and the support that reside in the Guru's sandals.

In the words of the Maharashtrian poet-saint Eknath Maharaj, "By the dust of my Guru's feet all the work was accomplished. Eknath has merged his mind in Shri Guru's feet. . . . By holding the feet of the Guru, all ignorance disappears. I have not performed cruel austerities, offered sacrifices, or wandered to sacred places. The means of all means is the feet of the Guru."[28]

NOTE *on* SOURCES

We gratefully acknowledge the following sources for permission to reprint quotations in this book.

Coleman Barks and Robert Bly, *Night and Sleep: Versions of Rumi* (Cambridge, Mass.: Yellow Moon Press, 1981).

Raimundo Panikkar, *The Vedic Experience: Mantramanjari* (London: Darton, Longman and Todd, 1977).

NOTES

Foreword

1. A *bīja* mantra represents the essential nature of an element or principle of creation: *lam*, earth; *vam*, water; *ram*, fire; *yam*, air; and *ham*, ether. These are located in the various chakras found at the base of the spine, in the sacral area, at the navel, the heart, and the base of the throat, respectively. The primordial sound *Om* is associated with the center between the eyebrows, and all syllables have their source in the *sahasrāra* at the crown of the head.

2. Each petal of a lotus or chakra represents a particular Sanskrit syllable. These are termed *āvarana*, or surrounding mantras of the central *bīja* mantra of the chakra.

3. In *khecharī mudrā*, the tongue curls back upward against the palate and into the nasal pharynx, opening the way to the *sahasrāra*.

Part One: The Guru

1. The Guru transcends the distinctions of male and female. In this book I refer to the Guru as "he" or "him" simply because of the conventions of English grammar. When I refer specifically to Gurumayi, I use the pronouns "she" or "her."

2. *Guru Gītā*, verse 89.

3. See *Shrī Dakshinamūrti Stotram*, verse 18 of "Arati," *The Nectar of Chanting* (South Fallsburg, N.Y.: SYDA Foundation, 1983), 136.

4. The four "great sayings" of the Upanishads are: "Consciousness is Brahman," from the *Aitareya Upanishad* of the *Rig Veda*; "This Self is Brahman," from the *Māndūkya Upanishad* of the *Atharva Veda*; "Thou art That," from the *Chāndogya Upanishad* of the *Sāma Veda*; and "I am Brahman," from the *Brihadāranyaka Upanishad* of the *Yajur Veda*.

5. *Mundaka Upanishad*, 1.2.12.

6. Jnaneshwar Maharaj, *Amritānubhava*, from an unpublished rendering by George Franklin, 2.13, 64, 65, 68.

7. *Guru Gītā*, verse 9.

8. Swami Muktananda, *From the Finite to the Infinite*, 2nd ed. (South Fallsburg, N.Y.: SYDA Foundation, 1994), 274-75.

9. Coleman Barks and Robert Bly, *Night and Sleep: Versions of Rumi* (Cambridge, Mass.: Yellow Moon Press, 1981), quoted on back cover.

10. Swami Muktananda, *From the Finite to the Infinite*, 513, 525.

11. Jnaneshwar Maharaj, *Amritānubhava*, 2.22.

12. Swami Muktananda, *In the Company of a Siddha*, rev. ed. (South Fallsburg, N.Y.: SYDA Foundation, 1985), 132.

13. Swami Muktananda, *From the Finite to the Infinite*, 36.

14. Raimundo Panikkar, *The Vedic Experience: Mantramanjari* (London: Darton, Longman and Todd, 1977), 96-97. *Rig Veda* 10.125.3, 4, 8.

15. Swami Chidvilasananda, *Kindle My Heart*, rev. ed. (South Fallsburg, N.Y.: SYDA Foundation, 1996), 197.

16. Swami Muktananda, *Kundalini: The Secret of Life*, 2nd ed. (South Fallsburg, NY.: SYDA Foundation, 1994), 7.

17. See *Kulārnava Tantra*, 14.15-34.

18. Swami Muktananda, *From the Finite to the Infinite*, 47.

19. *Kulārnava Tantra*, 13.51-52, 54.

20. Swami Muktananda, Swami Chidvilasananda, *Resonate with Stillness* (South Fallsburg, N.Y.: SYDA Foundation, 1995), July 31.

21. *Shiva Sūtra*, 3.28.

22. See *Brihadāranyaka Upanishad*, 2.4.5.

23. *Taittirīya Upanishad* 1.3.3.

24. Dr. Paul Muller-Ortega, foreword, *The Aphorisms of Shiva*, trans. with exposition and notes by Mark S. G. Dyczkowski (Albany: State University of New York Press, 1992), xi-xii.

25. Swami Muktananda, *From the Finite to the Infinite*, 212-13.

26. *Shiva Sambitā*, 3.11.

27. Swami Muktananda, *The Perfect Relationship* (South Fallsburg, N.Y.: SYDA Foundation, 1991), 67.

28. Swami Muktananda, Swami Chidvilasananda, *Resonate with Stillness*, August 19.

29. Swami Muktananda, *From the Finite to the Infinite*, 53.

30. Ibid.

31. Swami Chidvilasananda, unpublished talk, December 30, 1993.

32. Swami Vishnu Tirtha Maharaj, *Devātmā Shakti*, 1968 edition (Rishikesh: Muni ki Rati, 1948), 79-100. See also Swami Kripananda, *The Sacred Power* (South Fallsburg, N.Y.: SYDA Foundation, 1995), 62-79.

33. Swami Muktananda, *The Perfect Relationship*, 76.

34. Swami Muktananda, *Where Are You Going?* (South Fallsburg, N.Y.: SYDA Foundation, 1994), 64.

35. Swami Chidvilasananda, "Accepting Grace," *Darshan Magazine*, 27 (June 1989): 88, 91.

36. Swami Muktananda, *From the Finite to the Infinite*, 252.

37. Swami Muktananda, Swami Chidvilasananda, *Resonate with Stillness*, February 14.

38. Swami Muktananda, *Secret of the Siddhas* (South Fallsburg, N.Y.: SYDA Foundation, 1994), 67.

Part Two: The Guru's *Pādukās*

1. Swami Muktananda, *Satsang with Baba*, vol. 5 (Oakland, Calif.: SYDA Foundation, 1978), 53-54.

2. *Kulārnava Tantra*, 12.4-6.

3. Swami Muktananda, *Play of Consciousness* (South Fallsburg, N.Y.: SYDA Foundation, 1994), 72, 74.

4. *Darshan Magazine*, 46/47 (February 1991): 68.

5. Swami Muktananda, *From the Finite to the Infinite*, 234.

6. Swami Muktananda, *Lalleshwari* (South Fallsburg, N.Y.: SYDA Foundation, 1981), 39.

7. *Guru Gītā*, verse 45.

8. Swami Muktananda, *Nothing Exists That Is Not Śiva* (South Fallsburg, N.Y.: SYDA Foundation, 1997), 103.

9. *Prapañcha-sāra*, quoted by Kalicharana in his commentary on verse 43 of the *Shat Chakra Nirūpana*. This work is found in Sir John Woodroffe, *The Serpent Power*, 7th ed. (Madras: Ganesh and Company, 1964), 437.

10. *Guru Gītā*, verse 76.

11. Quoted in Swami Muktananda, *I Am That* (South Fallsburg, N.Y.: SYDA Foundation, 1992), 52.

12. Swami Chidvilasananda, unpublished talk, September 30, 1995.

13. See Sir John Woodroffe, *The Serpent Power*, 12th ed. (Madras: Ganesh and Company, 1981),481-500.

14. See *Shat Chakra Nirūpana*, verses 4, 14, 19, 22, 28, 32, and 40. See also Swami Kripananda, *The Sacred Power*, 81-109.

15. Swami Muktananda, *Mukteshwari* (South Fallsburg, N.Y.: SYDA Foundation, 1995), verses 927, 939, and 942.

16. See Swami Muktananda, *Play of Consciousness*, 96.

17. Kshemaraja, *Spanda Nirnaya*, a commentary on the *Spanda Kārikās*, 1.1.

18. *Guru Gītā*, verse 58.

19. *Pādukā Pañchaka*, verse 4.

20. *Pādukā Pañchaka*, verse 5.

21. Swami Muktananda, *Play of Consciousness*, 12.

22. *Lalitā Sahasranāma*, verse 106.

23. *Shiva Samhitā*, 5.103.

24. Swami Muktananda, *Satsang with Baba*, vol. 2, 241.

25. Ram Butler, *Siddha Yoga Correspondence Course*, vol. 8, lesson 34, 2-3.

26. Swami Muktananda, *Light on the Path* (South Fallsburg, N.Y.: SYDA Foundation, 1994), 45-46.

27. Swami Muktananda, *Satsang with Baba*, vol. 2, 22.

28. Peggy Bendet, "Eknath: A Life of Quiet Revolution." *Darshan Magazine*, 1 (June 1989): 26, 34.

GUIDE to SANSKRIT
PRONUNCIATION

～

For the reader's convenience, the Sanskrit and Hindi terms most frequently used in Siddha Yoga literature and courses appear throughout
the text in roman type with simple transliteration. *Śaktipāta*, for instance,
is shaktipat; *sādhanā* is sadhana, and so on. For less frequently used
Sanskrit words, the long vowels are marked in the text. The standard
international transliteration for each Sanskrit term is given in brackets
for glossary entries.

For readers not familiar with Sanskrit, the following is a guide for pronunciation.

Vowels
Sanskrit vowels are categorized as either long or short. In English transliteration, the long vowels are marked with a bar above the letter and are
pronounced twice as long as the short vowels. The vowels *e, ai, au,* and *o*
are always pronounced as long vowels.

Short:	Long:
a as in *cup*	*ā* as in *calm*
i as in *give*	*e* as in *save*
u as in *full*	*ī* as in *seen*
r as in *written*	*o* as in *know*
	ū as in *school*
	ai as in *aisle*
	au as in *cow*

Consonants
The main differences between Sanskrit and English pronunciation of
consonants are in the aspirated and retroflexive letters.

The aspirated letters have a definite *h* sound. The Sanskrit letter *kh*
is pronounced as in *inkhorn*; the *th* as in *boathouse*; the *ph* as in *loophole*.

The retroflexes are pronounced with the tip of the tongue touching
the hard palate; *t,* for instance, is pronounced as in *ant*; *d* as in *end*.

The sibilants are *ś, ṣ,* and *s*. The *ś* is pronounced as *sh* but with the
tongue touching the soft palate; the *ṣ* as *sh* with the tongue touching the
hard palate; the *s* as in *history*.

Other distinctive consonants are these:

c as in *church*	*ṃ* is a strong nasal
ch as in *pitch-hook*	*ḥ* is a strong aspiration
ñ as in *canyon*	

For a detailed pronunciation guide, see *The Nectar of Chanting,*
published by SYDA Foundation.

GLOSSARY

Aham brahmāsmi [*aham brahmāsmi*]
One of the four great sayings of Vedanta; it means "I am Brahman," the supreme Absolute. It occurs in the *Brihadāranyaka Upanishad* of the *Yajur Veda*.

A-ka-tha triangle [*a-ka-tha*]
A vibrating triangle in the *sahasrāra* composed of all the letters of the alphabet; the source of all sound.

Amritānubhava [*amṛtānubhava*]
Literally, "The Nectar of Self-Awareness"; a short work composed by the great poet-saint Jnaneshwar Maharaj.

Anāhata chakra [*anāhata cakra*]
The spiritual center located at the heart. The unstruck (*anāhata*) sound heard in meditation originates in this center.

Āratī [*āratī*]
A ritual act of worship during which a flame, symbolic of the individual soul, is waved before the form of a deity, sacred being, or image that embodies the divine light of Consciousness. *Āratī* is preceded by the sound of bells, conches, and drums, and accompanied by the singing of a prayer.

Āsana [*āsana*]
Various bodily postures practiced to strengthen the body and purify the *nādīs*. *See also* Nādī.

Ashram [*āśrama*]
A community where spiritual discipline is practiced; the abode of a saint or holy being.

Ashtānga yoga [*aṣṭāṅga yoga*]
Literally, the "eight limbs of yoga"; eight stages of yoga described by Patanjali in his *Yoga Sūtras*, the authoritative text on *raja yoga*. The eight stages are self-restraint, daily practices, steady posture, breath control, sense withdrawal, concentration, meditation, and union with the Absolute. *See also* Patanjali.

Avadhūta [*avadhūta*]
An enlightened being who lives in a state beyond body-consciousness and whose behavior is not bound by ordinary social conventions.

Ayodhya
The capital city of the Kosala kingdom of Dasharatha in the Indian epic the *Rāmāyana*.

Baba, Babaji [*bābā*]
A term of affection for a saint or holy man.

Bhakta [*bhakta*]
A devotee.

Bhakti [*bhakti*]
Devotion.

Bharata
In the Indian epic the *Rāmāyana*, a brother of Rama, born of Kaikeyi; he refused to rule during Rama's exile but lived an ascetic life in Nandigrama with Rama's sandals on the throne.

Bhastrikā [*bhastrikā*]
A form of *prānāyāma* known as "bellows breathing," in which the breath is drawn forcefully in and out. *See also* Prānāyāma.

Bindi [*bindi*]
An auspicious mark placed between the eyebrows, worn in remembrance of the Guru.

Bindu [*bindu*]
Dot or point; the Blue Pearl, a compact mass of *shakti* gathered into an undifferentiated point, ready to manifest as the universe. In the human being, it is the supracausal body. Also, in Sanskrit grammar, the *bindu* is a dot that is placed above a letter to give it a nasal resonance; the in-breath.

Blue Pearl. *See* Bindu.

Brahmamuhūrta [*brahmamuhūrta*]
The hours between 3:00 and 6:00 A.M., considered auspicious for the performance of spiritual practices.

Brahman [*brahman*]
Vedantic term for the absolute Reality.

Brahmanishtha [*brahmanistha*]
One who is "standing" or firmly established in the supreme Being, in Brahman, the absolute Reality; one of the qualifications of a Guru.

Brahmarandhra [*brahmarandhra*]
A subtle center located in the crown of the head at the fontanelle.

Darshan [*darśana*]
Seeing or being in the presence of a saint, a deity, or a sacred place.

Devi [*devī*]
The great Mother Goddess; Shiva's consort who represents *shakti*, or cosmic energy.

Devī Sūkta [*devīsūkta*]
Literally, "Hymn of the Goddess"; a hymn in the *Rig Veda* in which the Goddess describes Her true nature.

Dharma [*dharma*]
Essential duty; the law of righteousness; living in accordance with the divine Will. The highest dharma is to recognize the truth in one's own heart.

Dhyan Mandir
Formerly, the main meditation room in Gurudev Siddha Peeth; now Swami Muktananda's Samadhi Shrine.

Dīkshā [*dīkṣā*]
Initiation, the spiritual awakening of the disciple by shaktipat through a look, word, thought, or touch of the Guru.

Eknath Maharaj
(1528-1609) A householder poet-saint of Maharashtra, the author of several hundred *abhangas*, or devotional songs in the Marathi language.

Four bodies
The physical, subtle, causal, and supracausal bodies, which are experienced respectively in the states of waking, dream, deep sleep, and *turīya. See also* Bindu; Turīya.

Ganeshpuri
A village at the foot of Mandagni Mountain in Maharashtra, India. Bhagawan Nityananda settled in this region where yogis have performed spiritual practices for thousands of years. Gurudev Siddha Peeth, the ashram founded by Baba Muktananda at his Guru's command, is built on this sacred land.

Gunas [*guṇa*]
The three basic qualities of nature that determine the inherent characteristics of all created things. They are *sattva* (purity, light, harmony, goodness), *rajas* (activity, passion), and *tamas* (dullness, inertia, ignorance, darkness).

Guru [*guru*]
A spiritual Master who has attained oneness with God and who is therefore able both to initiate seekers and to guide them on the spiritual path to liberation. A Guru is also required to be learned in the scriptures and must belong to a lineage of Masters.

Gurudev Siddha Peeth
Siddha Peeth, literally "abode of the Siddhas." The main Siddha Yoga meditation ashram and the site of the Samadhi Shrine of Baba Muktananda. It was founded in 1956, when Bhagawan Nityananda instructed Swami Muktananda to live in a simple three-room dwelling near Ganeshpuri, India.

Guru Gītā [*gurugītā*]
Literally, "Song of the Guru"; an ancient Sanskrit text; a garland of mantras that describe the nature of the Guru, the Guru-disciple relationship, and meditation on the Guru. In Siddha Yoga meditation ashrams, the *Guru Gītā* is chanted every morning.

Guru tattva [*guru tattva*]
Literally, "Guru principle"; the essential teaching that God, the Guru, and the inner Self of all beings are one and the same thing.

Hamsa [*haṃsa*]
Literally, "I am That"; the natural vibration of the Self, which occurs spontaneously with each incoming and outgoing breath. By becoming aware of *Hamsa*, a seeker experiences the identity between his individual self and the supreme Self. Also repeated as *So'ham*. It is the name of the individual soul in the heart.

Jnaneshwar Maharaj
(1275-96) Foremost among the saints of Maharashtra and a child yogi of extraordinary powers. His verse commentary on the *Bhagavad Gītā*, the *Jñāneshwarī*, written in the Marathi language, is acknowledged as one of the world's most important spiritual works. He also composed a short work, the *Amritānubhava*, and over one hundred *abhangas*, or devotional songs in Marathi, in which he describes various spiritual experiences following the awakening of *kundalinī*.

Kashmir Shaivism
A nondual philosophy that recognizes the entire universe as a manifestion of *shakti*, the divine conscious energy. It explains how the formless, unmanifest, supreme Principle manifests as the universe.

Kriyās [*kriyā*]
Bodily movements caused by the awakened *kundalinī* in order to purify the body and nervous system.

Kulārnava Tantra [*kulārṇavatantra*]
Treatise on the practice of yoga; basic work of the Kaula school of tantrism.

Kumbhaka [*kumbhaka*]
Voluntary or involuntary retention of the breath.

Kumkum [*kumkum*]
A red powder used in Hindu worship; also worn as an auspicious mark between the eyebrows, in remembrance of the Guru.

Kundalinī [*kuṇḍalinī*]
The primordial Shakti, or cosmic energy, that lies dormant in a coiled form in the *mūladhara chakra* at the base of the spine. When She is awakened, She begins to move upward through the *sushumnā*, piercing the chakras and initiating various yogic processes that purify and rejuvenate the entire being. When She enters the *sahasrāra* at the crown of the head, the individual soul merges into the universal Self.

Lalitā Sahasranāma [*lalitā sahasranāma*]
Literally, "The Thousand Names of Lalita"; written in the form of a dialogue between the sage Agastya and the god Hayagriva, the text has evolved from the *Brahmānda Purāna*.

Lalleshwari
(1320-92) A fourteenth-century mystic and poet-saint from Kashmir.

Liberation
Freedom from the cycle of birth and death; the state of realization of oneness with the supreme Consciousness.

Maharashtra
A state on the west coast of central India. Many of the great poet-saints of India lived in Maharashtra, and the Samadhi Shrines of Bhagawan Nityananda and Swami Muktananda are there.

Mahāshūnya [*mahāśūnya*]
The Great Void. It is emptiness in the sense that it is without manifest creation. It is not a state of nonexistence because it has the nature of Being, Consciousness, and Bliss Absolute.

Mahāvākya [*mahāvākya*]
Literally, "great statements"; four statements containing the wisdom of the Upanishads, asserting the oneness of the individual Self and God. They are *prajñānam brahma*, "Consciousness is the Absolute"; *ayam ātma brahma*, "This Self is the Absolute"; *tat tvam asi*, "That thou art"; and *aham brahmāsmi*, "I am the Absolute."

Manana [*manana*]
Reflection, consideration. According to Advaita Vedanta, the path of knowledge consists of three steps: hearing the Guru's words (*shravana*), reflection on their meaning (*manana*), and meditating on them and imbibing their essence (*nididhyāsana*).

Mandala [*maṇḍala*]
Literally, "circle"; a sacred diagram composed of geometrical forms, where a deity is summoned and worshiped.

Mantra [*mantra*]
A name of God; a divine sound invested with the power to protect, purify, and transform the one who repeats it.

Māyā [*māyā*]
The power that veils and obscures the true nature of the Self and creates a sense of differentiation. It makes the universal Consciousness, which is One, appear as duality and multiplicity.

Nāda [*nāda*]
Inner divine music or sound heard during advanced stages of meditation.

Nādī [*nāḍī*]
A channel of the subtle body which carries the *prāna*, or vital force.

Nandigrama
In the Indian epic the *Rāmāyana*, the suburb of Ayodhya where Bharata lived an ascetic life during Rama's exile.

Nididhyāsana [*nididhyāsana*]
Meditation or contemplation; absorbing or imbibing the teachings; according to Advaita Vedanta, it is the third step in the process of receiving knowledge from the Guru. The first two steps are *shravana*, hearing the Guru's words, and *manana*, reflection on their meaning.

Nityananda
Eternal bliss; the name of Swami Muktananda's Guru.

Om [*oṃ*]
The primal sound, from which the entire universe emanates.

Om Namah Shivāya [*oṃ namaḥ śivāya*]
The mantra of the Siddha Yoga lineage, meaning "Salutations to Shiva," the inner Self. *Namah Shivāya* has five syllables and is called the *pañchāksharī* mantra.

Pādukā Pañchaka [*pādukā pañcaka*]
Literally, "Fivefold Footstool of the Guru"; a short text of seven

verses on the twelve-petaled lotus, which is inseparable from the pericarp of the *sahasrāra*.

Pādukās [*pādukā*]
Sandals worn or once worn by the Guru; *pūjā* is performed to them, and they are objects of the highest veneration.

Paramahamsa [*paramahaṃsa*]
The supreme Self in the *sahasrāra*.

Patanjali
A great sage of the fourth century and author of the famous *Yoga Sūtras*, the authoritative text of the path of *rāja yoga*.

Play of Consciousness
Swami Muktananda's spiritual autobiography, delineating the entire journey of Kundalini from Her awakening to Her final merging with Shiva.

Pradakshina [*pradakṣiṇa*]
Circumambulation of an auspicious object, a deity, or a holy being.

Prakriti [*prakṛti*]
Primordial nature; the basic stuff of which the material world is made.

Prāna [*prāṇa*]
The vital force.

Pranām [*praṇāma*]
To bow down before a deity or a holy being.

Prānāyāma [*prāṇāyāma*]
A yogic technique, consisting of the systematic regulation and control of the breath, that leads to steadiness of mind.

Pūjā [*pūjā*]
Worship; actions performed in worship; also, an altar with images of the Guru or deity and objects used in worship.

Purusha [*puruṣa*]
The individual soul, the experiencing subject.

Rajoguna. *See* Gunas.

Rāmāyana [*rāmāyaṇa*]
Attributed to the sage Valmiki, and one of the great epic poems of India. The *Rāmāyana* recounts the life and exploits of Lord Rama, the seventh incarnation of Vishnu. This story, so rich with spiritual meaning, has been told and retold down through the ages

by saints, poets, scholars, and common folk.

Rig Veda. *See* Vedas.

Rudra [*rudra*]
The Lord as destroyer, a form of Lord Shiva.

Rumi, Jalal al-Din
(1207-73): The most eminent poet-saint of Persia. After meeting Shams Tabrizi, an ecstatic wandering saint, he was transformed from a scholar into an intoxicated singer of divine love.

Sadhana [*sādhanā*]
The practice of spiritual discipline.

Sahasrāra [*sahasrāra*]
The thousand-petaled lotus at the crown of the head, the highest spiritual center in the human being, where the union of Shiva and Shakti takes place.

Sai Baba of Shirdi
(1838-1918): One of the great Siddhas of modern times. His Samadhi Shrine at Shirdi is a popular place of pilgrimage.

Samadhi Shrine [*samādhi*]
The final resting place of a great yogi's body. Such shrines are places of worship, permeated with the saint's spiritual power, and alive with blessings.

Samartha Ramdas
A seventeenth-century saint who was the Guru of King Shivaji and the spiritual inspiration behind the Maratha uprising against Mogul rule.

Samskāras [*saṃskāra*]
Impressions left by thoughts or actions in the past, which form our mental and emotional conditioning. They are stored in the *sushumnā*.

Sattvaguna. *See* Gunas.

Self
Divine Consciousness residing in the individual.

Seva [*sevā*]
Selfless service.

Shakti [*śakti*]
Spiritual power; the divine cosmic power that creates and maintains the universe; may be defined as the goddess Shakti.

Shaktipat [*śaktipāta*]
Descent of grace; the transmission of *shakti*, or spiritual power, from the Guru to the disciple.

Shiva [*śiva*]
The all-pervasive supreme Reality; also, one of the Hindu trinity of gods, who carries out the act of destruction or dissolution.

Shiva Samhitā [*śivasaṃhitā*]
A Sanskrit text on yoga which explains the practice of *āsanas*, *prānāyāma*, and *mudrās* in order to awaken *kundalinī*.

Shiva Sūtras [*śivasūtra*]
A Sanskrit text which Lord Shiva revealed to the sage Vasugupta. It consists of seventy-seven *sūtras*, or aphorisms, that were found inscribed on a rock in Kashmir.

Shiva Sūtra Vimarshinī [*śivasūtra vimarśinī*]
A commentary on the *Shiva Sūtras* by Kshemaraja.

Shravana [*śravaṇa*]
Hearing the words of the Guru; according to Advaita Vedanta, it is the first step in receiving the Guru's knowledge. The other two steps are *manana*, contemplating what has been heard, and *nididhyāsana*, meditating on the teachings and imbibing them.

Shree Muktananda Ashram
The international headquarters of the SYDA Foundation, established in 1979 in South Fallsburg, New York.

Shrotriya [*śrotriya*]
Literally, "learned in the scriptures"; one of the qualifications of a Guru.

Siddha [*siddha*]
A perfected Master; one who has attained the state of unity-awareness and who experiences himself as all-pervasive.

So'ham [*so'ham*]
Literally, "I am That." *See* Hamsa.

South Fallsburg, New York
The location of Shree Muktananda Ashram, established as the international headquarters of the SYDA Foundation in 1979.

Spanda Nirnaya [*spanda nirṇaya*]
A commentary by Kshemaraja on the *Spanda Kārikā*, an elaboration of the principles of the *Shiva Sūtras*.

Subtle body
An energy body interpenetrating the physical body; according to the *Prashna Upanishad*, the subtle body is composed of 720 million *nādīs*. It is the body in which we experience the dream state.

Sushumnā nādī [*suṣumṇānādī*]
The most important of all the *nādīs*, the central channel, which extends from the base of the spine to the crown of the head. It is the pathway of the awakened *kundalinī*.

Swami or **Swamiji**
A term of respectful address for a *sannyāsi*, or monk.

Taittirīya Upanishad [*taittirīyopaniṣad*]
An Upanishad of the *Yajur Veda*, dealing with the knowledge of the supreme Self.

Tamoguna. *See* Gunas.

Trimūrti [*trimūrti*]
The trinity of the Hindu tradition. They are Brahma, the creator; Vishnu, the preserver, or sustainer; and Shiva, the destroyer, the deity who reabsorbs the creation into Himself.

Tukaram Maharaj
(1608-50) A great poet-saint of Maharashtra born at Dehu, who composed thousands of *abhangas*, devotional songs in the Marathi language.

Turīya [*turīya*]
The fourth, or transcendental, state of consciousness, associated with the supracausal body, the *bindu* or Blue Pearl.

Vedas [*veda*]
The four ancient, authoritative Hindu scriptures, regarded as divinely revealed. The four Vedas are the *Rig Veda*, *Yajur Veda*, *Sāma Veda*, and *Atharva Veda*.

Visarga [*visarga*]
Emanation, creation; also, according to Sanskrit grammar, *visarga* consists of two dots written one above the other like a colon [:] at the end of a word, which give it a final aspiration, "h," the expulsion of the breath.

Yongquan
Literally, "gushing spring"; according to Chinese medicine, an acupuncture point in the sole of the foot.

INDEX

THE TRADITION of
SIDDHA YOGA MEDITATION

~

The spiritual unfoldment that is inspired by the grace and guidance of an enlightened master, known as a Siddha Guru, is the essence of the tradition of Siddha Yoga meditation.

A Siddha Guru is one who has the power and knowledge to give others the inner experience of God. Through the transmission of grace, known as shaktipat initiation, the Siddha master awakens a seeker's inner spiritual energy. Having walked the spiritual path to its final goal, Siddha Gurus dedicate their lives to helping others complete the same journey.

Swami Chidvilasananda, widely known as Gurumayi, is a Siddha Guru. Since early childhood, she has been a disciple of the Siddha master Swami Muktananda Paramahamsa (1908-82). It was he who invested Swami Chidvilasananda with the knowledge, power, and authority of the ancient tradition of Siddhas.

During his lifetime Swami Muktananda became adept at many of the classical paths of yoga, yet he said his spiritual journey did not truly begin until Bhagawan Nityananda, one of the great saints of modern India, awakened him to the experience of the supreme power within himself.

Bhagawan Nityananda chose Swami Muktananda as his successor and directed him to bring shaktipat initiation and the timeless practices of yoga to seekers everywhere. Gurumayi continues in her Guru's tradition, offering the teachings of the Siddhas and shaktipat initiation to seekers around the world.

Through the Siddha Yoga principal practices of meditation, chanting, contemplation, and selfless service, thousands of people from many different traditions and cultures have discovered within themselves the source of lasting happiness and peace: the awareness that we are not separate from God.

Swami Chidvilasananda

FURTHER READING

Published by SYDA Foundation

～

Kindle My Heart SWAMI CHIDVILASANANDA

The first of Gurumayi's books, this is an introduction to the classic themes of the spiritual journey, arranged thematically. There are chapters on such subjects as meditation, mantra, control of the senses, the Guru, the disciple, and the state of a great being.

Enthusiasm SWAMI CHIDVILASANANDA

"Be filled with enthusiasm and sing God's glory" is the theme of this collection of talks given by Gurumayi. In these pages, she inspires us to let the radiance of enthusiasm shine through every action, every thought, every minute of our lives. This, Gurumayi says, is singing God's glory.

Ashes at My Guru's Feet SWAMI CHIDVILASANANDA

In this priceless collection of poetry offered to her Guru, Swami Muktananda, Gurumayi generously shares with us her own experience of the spiritual path. In the universal language of poetry, Gurumayi portrays how the path of love for the Guru can burn the ego to ashes and open the disciple to purest light. *Illustrated.*

Resonate with Stillness: Daily Contemplations by SWAMI MUKTANANDA, SWAMI CHIDVILASANANDA

Every sentence of this exquisite collection of contemplations is an expression of wisdom and love from the Siddha masters Baba Muktananda and Gurumayi Chidvilasananda. The selections are dated and arranged in twelve themes of spiritual life, with a contemplation for each day of the year.

From the Finite to the Infinite SWAMI MUKTANANDA

This compilation of questions and answers is drawn from Baba's travels in the West. In it, he addresses all the issues a seeker might encounter on the spiritual path, from the earliest days until the culmination of the journey.

Play of Consciousness   SWAMI MUKTANANDA

In this intimate and powerful portrait, Baba Muktananda describes his own journey to Self-realization, revealing the process of transformation he experienced under the guidance of his Guru, Bhagawan Nityananda.

The Perfect Relationship   SWAMI MUKTANANDA

In this classic work, Baba Muktananda unravels the mystery of the sublime relationship between Guru and disciple.

Where Are You Going?   SWAMI MUKTANANDA

A comprehensive introduction to the teachings of Siddha Yoga meditation, this lively and anecdotal book explores the nature of the mind, the Self, the inner power, as well as mantra, meditation, and the Guru.

Mukteshwari   SWAMI MUKTANANDA

In a series of autobiographical aphorisms, Baba guides us through the stages of the spiritual path, inviting us to throw off our limitations and join him in the state of total freedom.

Kundalini: The Secret of Life   SWAMI MUKTANANDA

The awakening of *kundalinī*, the latent spiritual energy within us, marks the beginning of our journey to perfection. But what is the nature of this mighty force of transformation? How is it awakened? And how can its progress be nurtured? Baba Muktananda addresses these topics, which are so vital to every spiritual seeker.

Secret of the Siddhas   SWAMI MUKTANANDA

For thousands of years, the teachings of the Siddha masters have been handed down from Guru to disciple. Here Baba introduces us to the extraordinary lineage of Siddhas and interprets some basic tenets of Vedanta and Kashmir Shaivism, two philosophical schools at the heart of Siddha Yoga meditation.

Light on the Path   SWAMI MUKTANANDA

In this classic collection of six essays, Baba writes about the Guru's grace, the nature of God, the Guru-disciple relationship, divine love, mantra repetition, and the path of knowledge.

*You may learn more about the teachings and practices
of Siddha Yoga meditation by contacting:*

SYDA Foundation
P.O. Box 600, 371 Brickman Rd.
South Fallsburg, NY 12779-0600, USA

Tel: (914) 434-2000

or

Gurudev Siddha Peeth
P.O. Ganeshpuri, PIN 401 206
District Thana, Maharashtra, India

*For further information on books in print by
Swami Muktananda and Swami Chidvilasananda,
and editions in translation, please contact:*

Siddha Yoga Meditation Bookstore
P.O. Box 600, 371 Brickman Rd.
South Fallsburg, NY 12779-0600, USA

Tel: (914) 434-2000 ext. 1700

Call toll free from the United States and Canada:
888-422-3334

Fax toll free from the United States and Canada:
888-422-3339